MW01297224

UML Modelling for

Business Analysts

With Illustrated Examples

Table of Contents

Preface

UML modelling is one of the widely used techniques in the software development industry. Business analysts use this technique to develop the requirements to make it suitable for the technology team and customers alike.

After spending several years in the IT industry, we have realized that requirements (or incomplete or incorrect understanding of the requirements) have been one of the primary reasons for the failure of the software projects. This has been proven time & again by the CHAOS report published by Standish Group.

So the motivation to write this book is to provide a comprehensive, detailed and practical guide on requirements development to enable every business analyst conduct this phase efficiently.

This book deals with requirements development and its sub-phases with examples and case studies. We have selected UML diagrams as the modelling technique to explain and guide you through the entire process.

Requirements development phase comprises of multiple steps comprising of:

- Requirements Elicitation
- Requirements analysis and modelling
- Requirements specification and validation

Chapter 1 and 2 lays the foundation for the entire book. Chapter 1 provides fundamentals of software development life cycle methodology. Chapter 2 provides the basics of requirements development process in the overall context of SDLC.

As the focus is on UML modelling, chapter 3 to chapter 8 deals with UML modelling.

Chapter 9 deals with the requirements specifications and validation.

We have presented complete requirements specification document in two formats:

- System Requirements specification (SRS) document
- Use case specification document

We have also discussed structured analysis and design (SAD) methodology in the Appendix.

We have also used two case studies, in addition to examples, to explain the concepts practically.

Sandeep Desai

Abhishek Srivastava

1. Software Development Methodologies

INTRODUCTION

Software development methodologies better known as Software development lifecycles (SDLC) are the methodologies which are used to develop software applications. Several SDLC methodologies have been developed over the years, right from waterfall methodologies to now DevOps.

Every SDLC methodology comprises of phases. In some of the methodologies, the phases are conducted in a sequential manner, whereas in others they are carried out in incremental manner.

Broadly speaking, all the methodologies will comprise of the phases as shown in the image below:

Fig 1.1 Waterfall Development Methodology

Let's see what happens in each phase.

Requirement Development

Requirement development is probably the most important phase of any SDLC methodology. The key aspects of this phase are:

- Input: BRD (Business requirements document), Existing System Screens, Processes, Reports

- Questions, Interviews, meetings are conducted to get detailed requirements

- Requirements are analyzed, validated and documented

- Prototypes can also be developed in this phase

- Output -> SRS/FS (System Requirements document/Functional specifications)

In this phase, we may also use modeling techniques like UML modeling to better understand the requirements. In our course, we have covered use case, activity, sequence and state machine diagrams of UML v 2.5. It's not mandatory to create all the diagrams for all the projects, it depends on the suitability, complexity and timelines of the project.

Prototyping

A prototype is a dressed down version of a system. The prototypes have complete user interface developed with navigational aids but without any real coding. The prototyping phase helps in getting an agreement on the requirements from the customer.

Design

In this phase, technology team works out the approach for system implementation. Let's consider a simple example to understand the design phase. Consider the requirement of a screen to allow registered user to access authorized content. To achieve that, the technology team will work out the following:

- How does the login screen look like? What will be there on the screen like user id and password fields
- How will the user id and password be validated

The technology team works on "How things will be done?". As opposed to this, business analysts work on "What needs to be done?" during the requirements phase.

Coding

In this phase, the coding of the system is carried out. Based on the design document and program specification document, the project team carries out the coding. Developers are told well in advance about the coding standards to be followed. Many a times it has been observed that client also imposes their own standards for the codification. Developers are required to complete the Unit Testing (testing for each unit of code). Developers, before handing over the code to the Software development team, are expected to make detailed documentation of the code. Documentation must be lucid from the maintenance (further or future modifications) point of view.

Testing

Testing phase refers to the validation phase where the developed system gets tested against the expected system using test cases. The test cases are prepared by experts using the requirement agreement document (SRS document) and the business domain understanding. In the subsequent chapters we are going to have more discussions on this phase. Testing phase is to make sure that the delivered software is as per the customer expectations. The bench mark to make sure it is satisfying all the requirements is SRS (document which is released in the first phase).

System Implementation

Once the system is tested it is ready to go LIVE and the customer is expected to make all the arrangements to run the software. Large systems and business critical systems are tested sufficiently (like parallel runs or simulating real life situations etc.) to make sure that during implementation stage system will not break down. Systems implementation stage also involves extensive user training. Users are trained on the requisite business function of the software and asked to practice before launching of the system.

WATERFALL MODEL

Waterfall is one of the oldest SDLC methods and is a sequential methodology. On the other hand, AGILE is an example of incremental methodology, wherein phases are executed repeatedly and in small iterations.

Waterfall model can be visualized easily by looking at the car assembly line manufacturing. It is designed to be efficient and every step has a clearly defined entry and exit criteria. As you can see in the Fig 1.2, the real challenge for this type of process is that these are designed to move in one direction. In case of any defect or errors, going back is a challenging task.

Fig 1.2 Car Assembly Line

The pros and cons of this SDLC methodology is shown below in the table:

Pros	Cons
Easiest to understand	Does not model the real world
Easiest to implement	Too much documentation
Enforced discipline	Adjusting scope during the life cycle can kill a project
Document and deliverable driven	No working software is produced until late during the life cycle
Meant for smaller projects with well-defined requirements	High amounts of risk and uncertainty

Table 1.1 Waterfall methodology pros and cons

PROTOTYPING MODEL

Prototyping model is a variation on waterfall model and is developed to overcome the shortcomings of waterfall model. Prototyping model involves development of prototypes during the requirement phase and even the design phase to make sure that customers have a better understanding of the requirements and changes to the requirements are minimized.

Pros	Cons
Customer can see the product and its progress through prototype	Prototyping may take more than anticipated time as number of iterations is difficult to estimate
Useful, when requirements are not completely ready	It may still not be safeguard against future changes

Table 1.2 Prototyping Model pros and cons

SPIRAL MODEL

Spiral model is an incremental methodology and as opposed to waterfall, phases can be carried out repeatedly as opposed to sequential methodology like waterfall. In this model, requirements are divided into multiple parts and are taken up in an iterative manner. Typically each iteration is selected carefully based on the risks profile. Requirements, which have feasibility risks or any other risks, are taken up in earlier iterations.

Figure below shows the diagrammatic representation of SPIRAL Model.

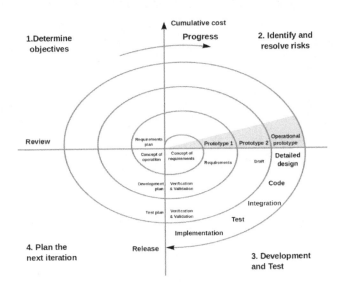

Fig 1.3 Spiral Model

Table shows the pros and cons of the Spiral model.

Pros	Cons
Good for large and mission-critical projects	Can be a costly model to use.
High amount of risk analysis	Risk analysis requires highly specific expertise.
Software is produced early in the software life cycle.	Not enough process documentation and guidelines available

Table 1.3 SPIRAL Model pros and cons

AGILE METHODOLOGY

AGILE methodology is one of the most popular methodologies these days. A lot of companies and projects are going the AGILE way. So what exactly is AGILE?

AGILE methodology is:

- Agile software development is a conceptual framework for software engineering that promotes development iterations throughout the life-cycle of the project.
- Software developed during one unit of time is referred to as an iteration, which may last from one to four weeks.
- Agile methods also emphasize working software as the primary measure of progress

Key AGILE Principles are:

- **Focus on Customer Value** – Align project, product and team visions to deliver better product quality – faster and cheaper.

- **Small Batches** - Create a flow of value to customers by "chunking" feature delivery into small increments.

- **Small, Integrated Teams** - Intense collaboration via face-to-face communication, collocation, etc; diversified roles on integrated, self-organizing, self-disciplined teams.

- **Small, Continuous Improvements** – Teams reflect, learn and adapt to change; work informs the plan.

What are the key characteristics of AGILE methodology?

- It's a Light Weight methodology
- It can work with small to medium sized teams
- It's highly recommended in vague and/or changing requirements scenario

One important aspect to note is that AGILE in itself is not a methodology, rather it represents a philosophy. There are various methods, which implement AGILE way of developing projects and these methodologies are:

- Extreme Programming ("XP")

- Agile Unified Process

- SCRUM

- Pair Programming

SCRUM

SCRUM is one of the most popular implementation methodologies for AGILE and in this book, we are going to discuss this methodology.

SCRUM is characterized by the following features:

- Self-organizing teams

- Product progresses in a series of month-long "sprints"

- Requirements are captured as items in a list of "product backlog"

- No specific engineering practices prescribed

- Uses generative rules to create an agile environment for delivering projects

- One of the "agile processes"

Figure on the next page shows the components of SCRUM:

Fig 1.4 SCRUM methodology

The SCRUM methodology has following components:

Requirements: User stories

Roles: Product Owner, Scrum Master, Team

Ceremonies: Sprint Planning, Sprint Review, Sprint Retrospective, & Daily Scrum Meeting

Artifacts: Product Backlog, Sprint Backlog, and Burndown Chart, User Stories

Let's look at each of these components in details.

User Stories

User Stories are probably the most important component of any SCRUM methodology. User stories are short, simple descriptions of a feature told from the perspective of the person who desires the new capability, usually a user or customer of the system. Typical format of a user story is

As a <type of user>, I want <some goal> so that <some reason>.

User stories are not usual SRS or FRD like documents. They are short and simple as the format shown above. These user stories are then written on sticky notes and then pasted on boards for ready reference as shown in the figure below:

Fig 1.5 User Stories on Scrum Board

Example of a user story is as follows:

<As a student I want to purchase a parking lot pass so that I can park my bike at the college parking lot>

Product Owner

Let's first look at the role of a Product Owner. The responsibilities of this role are as follows:

- Define the features of the product

- Decide on release date and content

- Be responsible for the profitability of the product (ROI)

- Prioritize features according to market value

- Adjust features and priority every iteration, as needed

- Accept or reject work results.

SCRUM Master

The SCRUM master's role and responsibilities are as follows:

- Represents management to the project

- Responsible for enacting Scrum values and practices

- Removes impediments

- Ensure that the team is fully functional and productive

- Enable close cooperation across all roles and functions

- Shield the team from external interferences

SCRUM Team

A SCRUM team, typically, comprises of 5-8 members and includes a product owner, a SCRUM master, developers and testers. Ideally the number of developers and testers should be equal. All the team members in a SCRUM team are full-time.

Having looked at the SCRUM team and the roles, lets now look at the key concepts relating to the SCRUM methodology.

Product Backlog

Product backlog represents the requirements or deliverables for the entire product. The key aspects of product backlog are as follows:

- It is managed and owned by a Product Owner

- It's a spreadsheet (typically) - A list of all desired work on the project

- It is usually created during the Sprint Planning Meeting

- It can be changed and re-prioritized

A product backlog contains the list of features along with the estimated effort and priority.

SPRINT

A SPRINT represents each iteration of the SCRUM methodology. Every SPRINT comprises of development, coding and testing phases. A SPRINT is:

- A month-long iteration

- NO outside influence can interfere with the Scrum team during the Sprint

- Each Sprint begins with the Daily Scrum Meeting

SPRINT Backlog

A SPRINT backlog is a subset of Product Backlog Items, which define the work for a Sprint. It is created ONLY by Team members of the SCRUM team. Each Item has its own status. It should be updated every day based on the discussions in the Daily scrum meetings. Typically SPRINTs don't have too many items/features. Each task is approximately 16 hrs long.

SPRINT backlog can be changed by the team whenever they need to, in order to meet the Sprint Goal. The change can also involve removing unnecessary tasks. Estimates for each item is also done whenever there's new information.

SPRINT Burndown Chart

SPRINT burndown chart depicts the total Sprint Backlog hours remaining per day. It shows the estimated amount of time to release the SPRINT. Ideally the SPRINT should burn down to zero to the end of the Sprint. The chart, as shown in the Fig below, is not a straight line.

Fig 1.6 SPRINT burndown chart

The burndown charts are also made for the entire product and in that case, the chart shows the burndown chart for the entire product, rather than just a SPRINT.

Ceremonies

Ceremonies in SCRUM refers to the meetings conducted. There are different types of meetings, which are conducted.

SPRINT planning meeting: It's a collaborative meeting, which is conducted in the beginning of each Sprint between the Product Owner, the Scrum Master and the Team. It takes 8 hours and consists of 2 parts ("before lunch and after lunch").

Kick-off meeting: It's a special form of Sprint Planning Meeting. It happens before the beginning of the Project.

Daily Standup/SPRINT meeting: As the name suggests, the daily standup meeting is a 10-15 minutes meetings and is generally conducted at the start of the day and following 3 questions are discussed during these meetings:

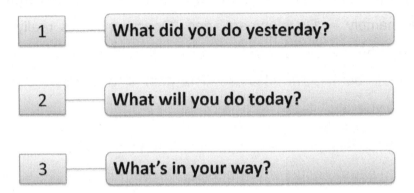

Fig 1.7 Daily Standup Meeting agenda

SPRINT Review Meeting: During this meeting, the team presents what it accomplished during the sprint. Typically it takes the form of a demo of new features or underlying architecture. It's an informal meeting and follows a 2-hour prep time rule. Typical participants of this meeting are:

- Customers
- Management
- Product Owner
- Other engineers

DEVOPS MODEL

DevOps is a term for a group of concepts that, while not all new, have catalyzed into a movement and are rapidly spreading throughout the technical community. DevOps originates from two words namely – "Development" and "Operations". It's really about bringing the developers and operations teams to work closely together to benefit the business. The goal is to reduce friction and increase velocity.

Typically development and operations team work in independent teams or *silos.* Focus of the operations team is to make sure that the systems don't go down – they are always up & running. The development teams are more creative and are focused on designing and developing the best solutions, even if it means delays.

So, what are the difference in views of development and operations teams?

Development team view

- Mostly delivers features after testing in development systems
- Dev system configuration and test data may not be same as production system
- Developers will have faster turnaround time w.r.t features

- Not much concerned about the infrastructural as well as deployment impact because of the code changes

Operations team view

- Worries more about PSR(Project Status Report) and Production Stability
- Rewarded mainly for uptime
- Lesser turnaround time w.r.t feature deployment and testing due to large number of dev builds coming their way
- Very much concerned about the infrastructural as well as deployment impact because of the code changes

Lot of companies like Google and Amazon, whose business models rely heavily or completely on software applications getting upgraded regularly with 99.99% uptime, can't afford to allow these two teams to work in silos. That has been the motivation for DevOps model to evolve.

Formally speaking, DevOps It's a software development methodology that stresses communication, collaboration and integration between developers and operations professionals thereby

- Enabling rapid evolution of products or services
- Reducing risk, improve quality across portfolio, and reduce

DevOps integration targets product delivery, quality testing, feature development and maintenance releases in order to improve reliability and security and faster development and deployment cycles.

How does DevOps bring together the development and Operations team:

- Developers work with Ops to understand the impact of code changes

- Developers now work more closely with production-equivalent systems

- Developers focus on metrics required by Ops team like PSR

- Ops now have more clarity on infrastructure needs

- More automation on deployment

- Closely monitors the Dev – Test – Prod pipeline for each deployment with immediate feedback

- Better collaboration and communication

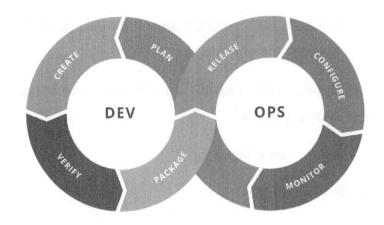

Fig 1.8 DevOps (Source: Wikimedia)

The adoption of DevOps is being driven by factors such as:

- Use of agile/other development processes and methodologies
- Demand for an increased rate of production releases from application and business stakeholders
- Wide availability of virtualized and cloud infrastructure from internal and external providers
- Increased usage of data center automation and configuration management tools

Principles of DevOps are:

– Collaborate across teams

– Develop and test in a production like environment

- Iterative and frequent deployments using repeatable and reliable processes

- Continuously monitor and validate operational quality characteristics

- Amplify feedback loops

Working of DevOps Model

DevOps extends the principle of AGILE and adds continuous delivery and Continuous deployment to achieve great results. In an Agile scenario, the development team produces working functionality at the end of every sprint. However, the completed functionality would have to wait until the release date arrives. Even on the release date, if the Ops team is not prepared for integration and deployment or business is not ready to go live with the new functionality, there will be release delays. Shorter time to market -- a key benefit of Agile -- is not fully realized. So, what are continuous deployment and delivery mechanisms?

Continuous Delivery

It's series of practices designed to ensure that code can be rapidly and safely deployed to production.

Continuous deployment

It's the next step of continuous delivery. Every change that passes the automated tests is deployed to production automatically.

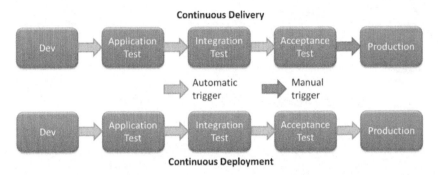

Fig 1.9 Continuous delivery and deployment

So, as we can see, by combining the AGILE development methodology with continuous deployment and delivery, we can achieve results, which are continuously being used by large organizations.

Benefits of DevOps Model

Cost
- 10% - 20% reduction in cost across end to end project delivery

Time to Market
- Up to 50% increase in time to market through process streamlining and automation

Delivery Risk
- Better quality and up to 30% reduction in defects in later test phases

Through put
- Increase in Productivity and more time for taking up new functionality

Fig 1.10 Benefits of DevOps

Real-life examples of DevOps Implementation

- Amazon deploys software upgrades every 11.6 seconds.
- Facebook deploys upgrades at least twice a day
- Netflix deploys upgrades a hundred times per day
- Flickr deploys upgrades 10+ times per day

These rapid and accurate deployments are next to impossible without the automated implementation of DevOps model. Are there tools, which can be used for DevOps? Yes, there are.

DevOps Tools

Let's look at these tools below:

- Deployment automation

  Fai , kickstart, preseed, cobbler

- Configuration Management

  Puppet, chef, cfengine, Bcfg2, Git, Ansible, SaltStack

- Continuous Integration/Build Automation

  Jenkins, maven, ant, cruisecontrol, hudson

- Continuous Deployment

  Puppet, Chef, Seren

- Application monitoring

  New Relic , Logstash, Bluepill, Nagios

SUMMARY

We have discussed software development methodologies in this chapter so far. These methodologies define, the order in which the phases of that methodology are executed in order to complete the software application. Some methodologies are sequential whereas others are incremental.

However, irrespective of the methodologies, the software design and development can be carried out using any of the two approaches:

- Structured Analysis and Design (SAD)
- Object Oriented Analysis and Design (OOAD)

OOAD has become the most popular approach because of its inherent superiority. *__We have provided a special section on SAD for your reference in the Appendix.__*

In the next chapter, we are going to discuss about requirement gathering and elicitation, first step of requirement engineering.

CHAPTER QUIZ

(Choose the right option. Only one answer is correct)

The process of understanding how an information system can support business needs, design the system, build it, and deliver it to users is known as:

1. Analysis phase of the SDLC
2. Object oriented approach
3. Systems development life cycle
4. None of these

One of the most important disadvantages(s) with the waterfall development methodology is:

1. It minimizes changes to the requirements as the project proceeds
2. It identifies system requirements long before programming begins
3. It is assumed that once a phase is over, it is frozen
4. None of these

The process of building new systems by combining packaged software, existing legacy systems, and new software written to integrate everything together is called _____.

1. Customization
2. Formal methodology
3. Outsourcing
4. Systems integration

Which one of the following is not an umbrella activity?

1. Project Management
2. Verification
3. Validation
4. Elicitation

The activity "User Acceptance Testing" is normally part of which phase of systems development?

1. Analysis and design
2. Implementation
3. Initiation
4. Maintenance

2. Requirements Development

Having discussed software development methodologies, let's dig deeper and focus on one of the key responsibility areas for a business analyst. Requirements engineering is one of the core responsibility areas for the business analyst.

REQUIREMENTS ENGINEERING

Requirement engineering deals with capturing, analyzing and managing the requirements throughout the lifecycle of the project. It consists of two distinct phases:

- Requirement Development
- Requirement Management

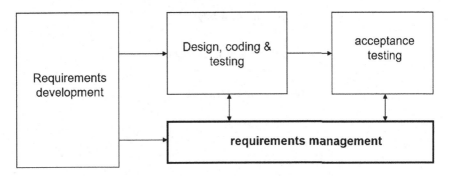

Fig 2.1 Requirement Engineering

As Fig 2.1 demonstrates, requirements development is followed by requirements management. Requirements development is the first phase for any software development project. Let's have a detailed look at the requirements development and management.

REQUIREMENTS DEVELOPMENT

Requirements development is the process of studying stakeholder needs to arrive at a set of complete and prioritized requirements that addresses strategy, people, process, and technology issues related to the project. Requirements development comprises of four steps as shown in figure below.

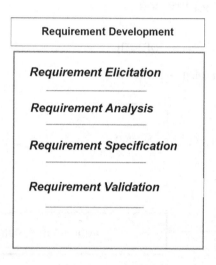

Fig 2.2 Requirements development phases

Let's look at the activities conducted during the requirements development phase.

Requirement Elicitation: It is the process of understanding the business requirements, context and the stakeholders. We will be discussing requirements elicitation in this chapter.

Requirement Analysis and Modelling: It is related to analyzing and modeling the requirements. We are going to discuss the techniques in chapter 3.

Requirement Specification and validation: It is about documenting the detailed requirement specifications in a functional specification (FS) or systems requirement specification (SRS) document. We are going to discuss this technique in chapter 9.

Once the requirements are documented in the previous phase, it is validated in this phase. In the validation phase, we look at incomplete, inconsistent, ambiguous requirements and eliminate them. We are going to discuss this technique in chapter 9.

REQUIREMENTS ELICITATION

As mentioned above, Requirements elicitation is the process of understanding the customer requirements, the context and stakeholders details. The output of this process is the functional specification (FSD) or system requirements specification (SRS) document.

Requirements elicitation phase comprises of multiple steps. These steps are as follows:

1. **Identifying and discovering the problem:** It starts with defining problem statement/description. A well-defined business problem should have the following:

   - Problem statement

   - Business context

   - Key Stakeholders

   - Success outcome

   - Potential Challenges

   - Scope

2. **Preparing for elicitation**

   - Identify the stakeholders

– Determine and choose the elicitation approaches

3. Conducting Elicitation

– Engage with stakeholders to gather requirements

Step 1 Identifying and discovering the problem: The first and the most important step is to understand and discover the problem, you as a business analyst are going to solve. A problem definition has certain key aspects that make the problem definition comprehensive and complete.

Let's look at a problem definition format:

What are we trying to achieve?

The basic problem we are trying to solve. It should be SMART: specific, measurable, action-oriented, relevant and time-bound.

What is the context for this system?
What is the current situation? What has happened so far? Why is this problem being addressed now?

Stakeholders Analysis
Who are the stakeholders or influencers for this project? What do they need?

How do you define the success for this project?
How will we measure the success of this project? What are the

parameters for the success

Where will we get more information?

How do we get more information for detailed understanding and documentation for this project

Step 2 Preparing for elicitation

Preparing for elicitation comprises of two steps:

- Identifying stakeholders
- Selecting the elicitation techniques

Identifying the stakeholders

Stakeholders are the drivers of every software project. Stakeholders can be from the customer team or from the IT company team.

Who is a stakeholder? International Institute of Business Analysis (IIBA) defines stakeholders as:

"A stakeholder is an individual or group that a business analyst is likely to interact with directly or indirectly"

Stakeholders influence the project in many ways. They are either sign-off authorities or they are end users of the project or they are the creators of the project. But most importantly, the customer stakeholders are the people, who participate in the requirements elicitation process.

The stakeholders can be any one from the following categories:

- business analyst
- customer
- domain subject matter expert
- end user
- implementation subject matter expert
- operational support
- project manager
- regulator
- sponsor
- supplier
- tester

The categories listed above is a representative list and there could be other categories as well.

Selecting the elicitation techniques

Requirements elicitation is the process of engaging the stakeholders to get the requirements. There are multiple requirements elicitation techniques, which are used. Some of the most important elicitation techniques are as shown in the Fig 2.3.

Fig 2.3 Elicitation Techniques

The choice of a specific technique will vary based on the type of application, the skill and sophistication of development team, the scale of the problem, the criticality of application, the technology used, the uniqueness of the application.

Following chart is a guide to for selecting requirement elicitation technique for any project:

Technique	Applicability	Advantages	Disadvantage
Interviewing &	In case of large group of users	Good understandi ng and	Time consuming

questionnaire	available	better conclusion can be drawn	Sometimes lot of chaos
Requirement workshop	Things are not clear. Users are not on same platform	Well defined group Less time consuming	Biased opinion (depends upon group selected for workshop)
Brainstorming and idea reduction	Large number of people (more than 15)	More analysis, evaluation of concepts	Sometime cannot come to any conclusion
Storyboards	In case of medium number of people available with few ideas	Micro level analysis of each idea	Sometimes it can go away from subject.

Prototyping	In case of product development, concept development and approach development	Helps in taking feedback from users. No effort loss after developing product 1st approach: Develop product with "critical" points and discuss with user 2nd approach: Develop screens and discuss with	Sometimes time consuming

		user to	
		understand	
		user taste	

It's quite common to use more than one techniques during the requirements elicitation phase. During the requirements elicitation process, using any of the techniques mentioned above, the business analyst(s) identifies the features or functions of the system and develops it to make it suitable for the development team to take it forward.

REQUIREMENTS ANALYSIS & MODELLING

The requirements elicitation phase is followed by requirements analysis ad modelling. During the requirements elicitation phase, stakeholders explain the requirements of the software system, to be developed. The requirements are analyzed and modelled to understand them better and to be able to make them suitable for the development team's understanding.

Requirements analysis and modelling is a multi-step process and we are going to discuss these steps in details in chapter 3.

UML Modelling is one of the techniques for requirements analysis and modelling. Data Flow diagrams (DFD) modelling is another technique used for requirements analysis and modelling. We have provided an overview of DFD modelling in Appendix.

REQUIREMENTS SPECIFICATIONS AND VALIDATION

The detailed requirements are captured and documented in a specifications document. The specifications document format and structure is decided mutually between the customer and the IT company managers.

The formal specifications document are typically template based and some of the most common specifications document used in the IT industry are:

- System Requirements Specifications (SRS) Document
- Functional specifications document (FSD)

Once the requirements specifications are created, it is verified and validated. Verification and validation of requirements ensure that these requirements meet the expected quality expectations.

From the next chapter onwards, we are going to dig deeper and discuss the requirements analysis and modelling process using UML diagrams. These steps are discussed from chapter 3 to chapter 7. In chapter 8, we are going to discuss requirements specifications and validation.

SUMMARY

We have discussed requirements development phase in this chapter. Requirements development phase comprises of multiple steps as listed in this chapter. It comprises of requirements elicitation, requirements analysis and modeling and requirements specifications and validation.

The focus of this book is to provide a comprehensive and practical guide to requirements development phase using UML diagrams also known as UML modelling.

We are going to describe the steps of requirements analysis and modelling with UML in the next chapter followed by detailed chapters on specific UML diagrams like use cases, activity diagram, sequence diagram etc.

CHAPTER QUIZ

(Choose the right option. Only one answer is correct)

The information gathering technique that is most effective in combining information from a variety of perspectives, building consensus, and resolving discrepancies is:

1. Document analysis
2. Observation
3. Interviews
4. Requirements Workshop

The information gathering technique that enables the analyst to collect facts and opinions from a wide range of geographically dispersed people quickly and with the least expense is the _____.

1. Requirements Workshop
2. Observation
3. Interviews
4. Questionnaire

Requirements represent an external view of any system. State whether this statement is TRUE or FALSE

1. TRUE
2. FALSE

Choose the technique, which is not a valid requirements elicitation technique

1. Brainstorming
2. Interviews
3. Questionnaire
4. Prototyping

Requirements engineering process includes two sub processes, select the correct combination

1. Requirements development and requirements traceability
2. Requirements development and requirements management
3. Requirements development and requirements elicitation
4. Requirements elicitation and requirements specifications

3. Requirement Analysis and Modeling with UML

In the previous chapter, we discussed requirements development broadly and the requirement elicitation specifically. Once the requirement gathering process starts, its objective is to gather a detailed, in-depth and correct understanding of the requirements.

Analysis and Modeling work in tandem to help us have a thorough understanding of the requirements.

In this chapter, we are going to look at the requirements analysis and modelling process using UML diagrams. There are several UML diagrams as per UML specifications 2.5, however as a business analyst, you will be using a few of the UML diagrams like use case, activity diagrams, sequence diagrams and class diagrams. State machine diagrams can also be used sometimes but it's not very common and we have not covered state machine diagrams in this book.

WHAT IS REQUIREMENT ANALYSIS?

What does analysis mean? Why do we conduct analysis?

"Separation of any material or abstract entity into its constituent elements"

"Analysis process is the method of studying the nature of something or of determining its essential features and their relations"

The literal meaning of analysis indicates that analysis is the method of understanding something by looking at its components (or what's it made up of). In software development lifecycle methodology also, requirements analysis is conducted to understand the functional requirements and their relationships. This helps in understanding the system better.

Requirements analysis is an approach rather than a technique. During the analysis process, we use a combination of techniques, which includes decomposition, abstraction and visual modelling.

Decomposition refers to the breaking down of a system into its constituent elements. The decomposition may take place in more than one step, as we are going to understand with the help of a case study and illustrated example.

Abstraction is a technique to identify concepts or patterns from the details. A simple example of abstraction is to think of a phone number. On the face of it, a phone number like +912228574976 is just a number. However, on closer look, we can conceptualize that – a phone number comprises of 4 structures as shown below:

- ISD Code
- STD Code
- Area Code
- Phone Number

This understanding helps in designing a software system, which is scalable and robust.

Modelling is all about creating visual diagrams to represent the elements of a system. A visual model could be made to represent the structure of the system or to represent a business process (Flowcharts are used to model a business process).

Let's understand these concepts with the help of a case study.

WHAT IS MODELLING?

A picture is worth a thousand words.

Visual representation of a concept or a thought is the best way to understand the concept or a thought. It helps in visualizing the final product.

In automobile industry, a new car concept is modelled and discussed before deciding to go ahead with the production. Sometimes they present the concept in trade shows and exhibitions as well to get first hand reaction and feedbacks from the customers. This way, they can make a more informed decision to go ahead with the production, setting up a production facility is a major investment.

Space, real estate, toy and many other industries make extensive use of visual modelling to make smart choices.

Software development is no different and we have used several modelling techniques. Some of the modelling techniques are as follows:

- UML Modelling
- DFD Modelling
- Prototyping

In this book, we have not only discussed UML modelling as a visual modelling technique, but have also discussed at length, using UML modelling as part of requirements analysis and modelling, one of the key responsibility areas for a business analyst.

PROTOTYPING AS A MODELING TOOL

There could be multiple ways of modeling a system

In this chapter, we are going to give you a brief overview of prototyping as a modeling tool.

Prototyping is a modelling technique, which enables business analysts to understand the requirements. It also helps the customer in having better clarity on – what are they looking for? Prototyping is the not the only modelling technique available as discussed in this book.

While in the requirements phase, prototyping or rapid prototyping can take many different forms. The main purpose is to quickly construct a prototype of the system and use it to acquire customer/users' feedback.

The simplest prototype could be a set of drawings that illustrate the user interfaces of the future system. The most sophisticated prototype could be a partially implemented system that the users can experiment with to gain hands-on experience. The most commonly seen prototype is one that the team can demonstrate to the customer. These prototypes are demonstrated to seek an agreement on the functionality and user interfaces of the system.

Which type of prototype to use is an application dependent issue? For instance, applications that are mostly concerned with mission critical operations would benefit from prototypes that demonstrate the functionality and behavior. Applications that are end user oriented would benefit from prototypes that demonstrate the user interfaces.

Types of prototypes

There are two types of prototypes- Throwaway and Evolutionary Prototype.

Throwaway Prototyping

Throwaway prototyping refers to a type of prototype, which is not used once it serves it purpose. The purpose of creating a prototype is to reach an agreement on the requirements in details. Since this type of prototype is not re-usable, a quick prototyping methodology is used. There are tools available, which enables quick prototyping. However, it's not uncommon to use quick prototyping using pencils and pens on white paper sheets.

Evolutionary prototyping

As opposed to throwaway prototyping, evolutionary prototyping is a re-usable technique. We plan and approach creation of prototypes so that they can be used by the development team as well.

Typically, this kind of prototyping requires a more sophisticated tool and most of the development environment have these capabilities.

Creating prototypes is relatively easier tasks and several tools are available, which can be used to create screens quickly. You don't need any technical skills to do so. Here are some examples, which we created using Pencil, a prototyping tool:

Fig 3.1 Prototype screen

Fig 3.2 Prototype screen

REQUIREMENTS ANALYSIS AND MODELLING PROCESS

In the previous sections, we discussed requirements analysis and modelling concepts with examples. Requirements analysis and modelling is a part of the requirements development phase of software development. As our focus in this book is UML modelling, let's now understand the overall process of requirements analysis and modelling using UML.

Fig ... illustrates and refreshes the software development phases and the context of requirements analysis and modelling. We have discussed the steps of requirements elicitation in chapter 2.

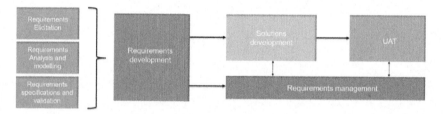

Fig 3.2 SDLC and Requirements analysis and Modelling

Let's look at the complete requirements development process before we start delving into individual steps. The requirements development process comprises of the following steps:

Step 1: Requirements elicitation

This step comprises of following activities:

- Identifying and discovering the problem
- Preparing for elicitation
- Conducting Elicitation

Requirements elicitation step has already been discussed in details in chapter 2.

Step 2: Requirements Analysis and Modelling

This step comprises of the following activities. These activities are done iteratively.

- Identify structural elements/functions – use decomposition & abstraction (This chapter)
- Identify use cases & Create use case model (Chapter 5)
- Identify Scenarios (Chapter 6)
- Create Activity diagrams (Chapter 6)
- Create sequence diagram, if needed (Chapter 7)
- Identify Classes and build logical data model (Chapter 8)

We are going to discuss requirements analysis and modelling activities in this and subsequent chapters.

Step 3: Requirements Specifications and validation

This step comprises of the following activities:

- Creating a specifications document (SRS, FSD, Use case specifications etc)
- Conducting verification and validation on specifications document

We are going to discuss this step in chapter 9.

Identify structural elements/functions

During requirements elicitation, we engage and collaborate with the customer stakeholders to gather requirements. During this process, it's important to understand the big picture.

Defining the problem and the goal provides us the overall business objective and the reasons for the proposed software. Having understood the business goal, the next step is to start understanding the system. What's the big picture? How do the parts of the system fit together? Where does this software fit into the overall organizational software infrastructure?

This approach to understand the system is also referred to as top-down approach as opposed to bottom-up approach. In bottom-up approach, we look at a system from grounds up, by looking at small pieces of the proposed system.

Decomposition and abstraction helps us in understanding the overall structure of the system. We discussed about these concepts in the beginning of this chapter.

Let's look at a case study to understand this activity.

CASE STUDY

Mobile Banking System

A new age bank Incarta Development bank is planning to launch its mobile banking app. The bank plans to provide following banking operations on the mobile app with adequate level of security.

The bank is intending to allow its customers to use features related to the following divisions:

- Retail Banking
- Home Loans
- Credit Cards
- Mutual Funs

The services, which the bank is planning to offer to its customers are as shown below:

- View Bank Balance
- Funds transfer
- Credit Card Bill payment
- Home loan amortization schedule

The bank is based in multiple cities across India.

The requirements analysis and modelling is an iterative process. We start by creating models of the system to analyze and to understand it better.

In the first, Iteration, we can create the model based on the given information as shown below:

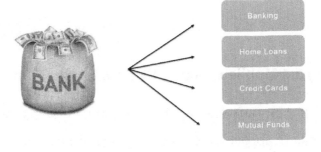

Fig 3.3 Mobile Banking System function Structure

In the above diagram, we have modelled the given information visually. The next diagram shows the further analysis and representation of its constituents as shown in the next diagram:

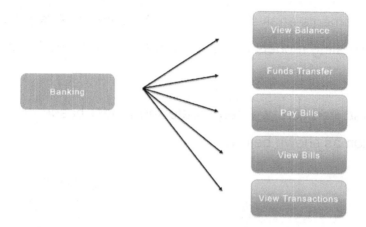

Fig 3.4 Mobile Banking System function Structure

The second diagram shows the banking services offered on the mobile banking application. This diagram, paves the way for further discussions with the customer to understand each of the services and its details. I have shown the information gathered from the customer on *funds transfer service* as shown in the diagram:

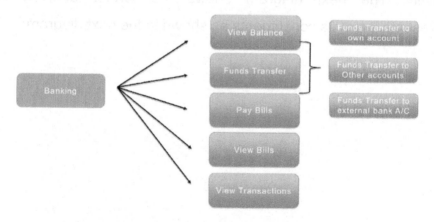

Fig 3.5 Mobile Banking System function Structure

As we start brainstorming and digging deeper, we start getting more details of each feature/function. Once we have understood the key functions and features, we start the use case modelling. We are going to discuss the use case modelling in chapter 5. In chapter 4, we are going to have a detailed look at UML as a modelling language.

SUMMARY

This chapter is a critical part of this book as it lays the foundation for understanding the requirements analysis and modelling process in the overall context. We have explained the concepts of requirements analysis and modelling in the first part of this chapter.

In the next chapter, we have looked at the requirements development process steps. Requirements analysis and modelling is part of requirements development process.

Finally, we have looked at the first activity in the requirements analysis and modelling step. In this step, we try and understand the big picture of the proposed system. This helps us in understanding the relationships amongst the components of the system and its overall relationship to the other systems in the organization.

Last but not the least, we have started with a case study, which will be used throughout this book to help you understand the process better and appreciate the gradual development of requirements into detailed specifications.

CHAPTER QUIZ

(Choose the right option. Only one answer is correct)

Requirements analysis and modelling is a part of the following phase:

1. Requirements development
2. Requirements Management
3. Requirements specification
4. None of these

Requirements engineering comprises of the following sub-processes:

1. Requirements Development and specifications
2. Requirements specifications and validation
3. Requirements development and management
4. None of these

Evolutionary prototypes is different from throwaway prototypes because

1. It can be re-used
2. It is created using a tool only
3. None of these

4. Unified Modeling Language (UML)

Unified modeling language is a modeling language with a rich set of graphical notations and diagrams to represent and depict every aspect of software development and design process.

At the time of this book going to press, the latest version of UML is 2.5 and there are 14 diagrams specified by OMG (Object management group), the organization behind UML.

UML specifications categorizes the diagrams into two categories:

- Structural diagrams
- Behavior diagrams

Structure diagrams are meant for showing the structure of the system and its parts at different levels and for different phases. These diagrams don't show any form of interactions between the elements of the diagrams.

Behavior diagrams are interactive diagrams and are meant to show the interactions between the elements of the diagrams.

The tables below shows the structural and behavioral diagrams as per UML 2.5.

UML Diagram	Description
Class Diagram	This diagram shows the classes, relationship between the classes and the various attributes for the classes
Object Diagram	Objects are instances of classes and it represents relationship between the objects and the various attributes for the objects
Package Diagram	It shows the packages (logical grouping of classes, objects and other elements) and the relationship between the packages, if there are many packages in a system
Composite Structure Diagram	
Component Diagram	It shows components and dependencies between them. This type of diagrams is for modeling Service Oriented architecture (SOA) projects.
Deployment Diagram	Deployment diagrams could be used to show logical or physical **network architecture** of the system.
Profile Diagram	Profile diagrams are used to create diagrams which extend the existing diagrams

Table 4.1 Structural Diagrams

Example of a class diagram is shown below, as you can see that the class diagrams shows the structure of a system:

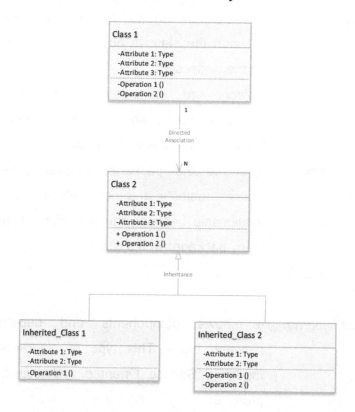

Fig 4.1 A class Diagram

UML Diagram	Description
Use Case Diagram	Use case diagrams represent a set of actions that users of the system can perform in the system. The users are referred to as Actors and

	the actions are known as use cases.
Activity Diagram	Activity diagrams are similar to flow charts as they show the series of steps, required to complete a task
State Machine Diagram	An object in a system can go through multiple states and these changes/transitions are shown in a state machine diagram.
Sequence Diagram	Most common kind of interaction diagrams which focuses on the message interchange between lifelines (objects).
Communication Diagram	Focuses on the interaction between **lifelines** where the architecture of the internal structure and how this corresponds with the **message** passing is central.
Timing Diagram	Shows interactions when a primary purpose of the diagram is to reason about time. Timing diagrams focus on conditions changing within and among lifelines along a linear time axis.
Interaction Overview Diagram	Defines interactions through a variant of activity diagrams in a way that promotes overview of the control flow.

Table 4.2 Behavior diagrams

We are going to discuss the following diagrams, as these are relevant from a business analyst's perspective:

- Use Case diagram
- Activity Diagram
- Sequence diagram
- Class Diagram

However, use case and activity diagrams are used more frequently than the other diagrams because of their complexity.

UML TOOLS

There are a number of tools available in the market, which can be used for UML modeling. Some of the tools are commercial products, with case tools like features, whereas some of them are open source tools, which provide basic UML modeling features.

In this section, I have reviewed 3 tools. Two of which are free tools, whereas the third one is a commercial tool – Microsoft Visio.

Microsoft Visio

Microsoft Visio is a commercial tool. It is a general purpose tool for creating variety of diagrams. It also has the capability to create UML diagrams.

To work with MS Visio, you need to select the category from a big list of diagrams categories available as shown in the Fig 4.2.

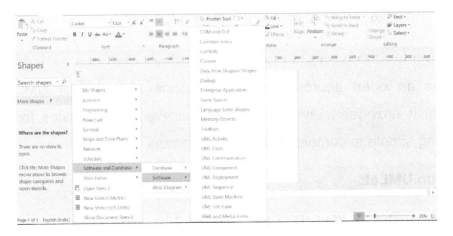

Fig 4.2 MS Visio

Once you select a category, Visio displays all the available symbols for that category. Fig 4.3 shows the diagrams available if we choose **UML use case** from the category.

Fig 4.3 Use case symbols in Visio

The canvass is represented by a white rectangular area, where you can drag the symbols from the left. The symbols are editable and you can change the names and properties as desired.

UMLet

UMLet is an open source tool and supports all types of UML diagrams. It provides individual elements as well as templates for developing simple to complex sequence diagrams.

Setting up UMLet:

To set up UMLet on your machine, you need to follow the following steps.

Step1

Visit the URL http://www.umlet.com/changes.htm and download the latest version of UMLet. As on today the latest version of UMLet is version 14.1.1 as shown in the screenshot below:

Fig 4.4 UMLet Download

Click on the UMLet 14.1.1 and download the ZIP file.

Step 2

Go to the folder where you downloaded the zip file. Unzip the files to a desired folder. Once it is unzipped, go to the folder and you can see the following directory structure:

Name	Date modified	Type	Size
custom_elements	1/14/2016 5:14...	File folder	
html	6/3/2015 7:58 ...	File folder	
img	1/14/2016 5:12...	File folder	
lib	1/14/2016 5:14...	File folder	
palettes	1/14/2016 5:14...	File folder	
sourcefiles	6/3/2015 7:58 ...	File folder	
LICENCE.txt	1/14/2016 5:12...	Text Document	35 KB
umlet.desktop	1/14/2016 5:12...	DESKTOP File	1 KB
Umlet.exe	1/14/2016 5:12...	Application	62 KB
umlet.jar	1/14/2016 5:14...	Executable Jar F...	43 KB
umlet.sh	1/14/2016 5:12...	Shell Script	1 KB

Fig 4.5 UMLet Download

Double-click on the Umlet.exe and it will open the UMLet tool and you can see the following screen:

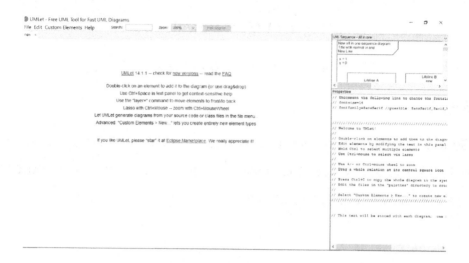

Fig 4.6 UMLet

Web Sequence Diagrams (Web based tool)

WebSequenceDiagrams.com is a free web based tool. It's my personal favorite as I find it extremely easy to create sequence diagrams. Sequence diagrams are probably the most complicated UML diagrams. This tool allows us to create the sequence diagrams using *simple English lie scripts*.

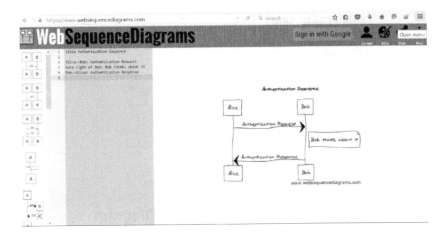

Fig 4.7 Web Sequence Diagrams

Styles available in web sequence diagram tool

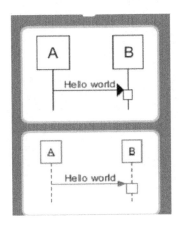

Fig 4.8 Web Sequence Diagrams Styles

The script has a title element, providing the title of the diagram, as shown in the diagram above.

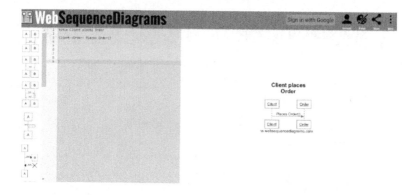

Fig 4.9 Creating Sequence Diagram

SUMMARY

In this chapter, we looked at the Unified modelling language specifications. We looked at the diagrams, which are important from a business analyst perspective.

There are multiple tools for creating UML diagrams with varying degree of complexity. We have discussed 3 tools in this chapter:

- UMLet, which is an open source UML modelling tool.
- WebSequenceDiagrams, it is again a free but completely online tool, which helps to draw sequence diagram using scripts only.
- MS Visio, it is one of commercial tools yet very powerful and popular tools

CHAPTER QUIZ

(Choose the right option, only one option is correct)

Which of the following UML diagrams has a static view?

1. Use case
2. Activity Diagrams
3. Sequence Diagrams
4. None of these

Structural diagrams emphasize the things that must be present in the system being modeled.

1. TRUE
2. FALSE

Class diagrams are used to represent data models, Is this statement correct?

1. Yes
2. No

Unified modelling language comprises of:

1. Only diagrams and symbols
2. Diagrams, symbols and scripting language

The UML 2.5 specifications has how many diagrams:

1. 13
2. 14
3. 15

5. Use case diagrams

INTRODUCTION

Use Case diagrams represent the features/functionality expected to be provided by the proposed system. However, the better way to understand use case diagrams is to think of use cases as – something that shows the way external entities use the system. The external entities are known as roles/actors, while the way they use the system are knows as use cases.

Illustrated Example – Actor & Use case

Consider the simple requirement given by a customer:

Only Registered users can login into the system

<u>Who is the actor here?</u>
Registered users are actors here. They are expected to login into the system.

<u>What is the use case here?</u>

To find the use case, just look at what does the actor do? The actor in this case (registered user) is expected to login into the system. So *login into the system* is the use case here.

Use Cases are used in the requirements Analysis phase of software development to articulate the high-level requirements of the system. The primary goals of Use Case diagrams include:

- Providing a high-level view of what the system does
- Identifying the users ("actors") of the system
- Determining areas needing human-computer interfaces.

Use cases are written for customer stakeholders, so care must be taken to ensure it's written in the language customer understands.

USE CASE SYMBOLS

Use case diagrams are simple diagrams yet they have elements which can also represent finer details. In this section, we are going to look at the elements of the use case model.

<u>Actor</u>

An Actor, as mentioned above, is an external entity which uses the system. An actor is represented by a stick figure as shown. Even though the image may indicate that an actor is a human being, but that's not always correct. Even a software system can be an actor. Any external system or human being, which receives data from the system or provides data to the system can be an actor for the system.

Please note that actor symbol may be different in different tools. Like Microsoft Visio uses following symbol for actors:

Bank Customer

Fig 5.1 Actor

WHO IS NOT AN ACTOR?

By definition, any entity which interacts with the software application (which is being developed) may be classified as an actor. The actors can be human beings, an external system or even a government organization or a regulatory body.

Who is not be considered as an actor? The obvious answer is – an entity which does not interact with the software system. Are there any entities which do interact with the system but are not considered as an actor? Yes, internal entities are not considered to be actors.

Consider the case of the database being used by the system to save data. Can that be an actor, no? Even though the data base is interacting with the software, it is not considered to be actor because it is internal to the system.

To summarize, any entity which interacts with the system and is external to the system is considered to be an actor.

USE CASES

A use case represents the functionality or feature of the proposed system. An actor interacts with the system through these identified use cases.

E.g. A user logging into the system, a user registering with a website or an accountant generating an invoice from the system.

Best practices for creating use cases

Use cases represent the functionality of a system from a user perspective. While writing the use cases, we should use action verbs. So, instead of writing "login screen", we should write "Login into the system".

So, what's the difference?

The difference is the way it is read. Use cases are written for customer stakeholders and it's a high level representation of the requirements. So saying *a registered user will login into the system* makes a lot of sense to the customer, isn't it?

Always start the use case with a verb and write the use cases from a user perspective rather than a development team perspective

Illustrated Example – Use case model

Consider the simple requirement:

A visitor makes a payment to complete the order.

This single statement surprisingly leads to two features, thereby two use cases.

- Make a payment
- Completing an order

The use case model with the actor for **make a payment** use case is as shown below:

Fig 5.2 Simple use case model

As you can see above, the use case "Makes a payment" is depicted by 3 elements. The first element is the actor "Visitor", the second element being use case "Makes a payment" and the third element is the association between the actor and the use case. The line connecting the actor and the use case is a simple association.

ACTORS

Actors can be categorized as primary and secondary actors. Primary actors are those external entities, who initiate the use case. Whereas secondary actors are those entities, who get involved in the use case passively. Secondary actors help the primary actors in completing the use case.

Illustrated Example – Reviewing Loan Application

In this simple example, we will look at a loan officer reviewing the loan application of a customer. This process also involves a quick round of credit rating for the customer.

This feature of the application is shown in the use case diagram below:

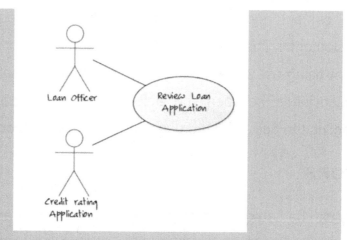

Fig 5.3 Review Loan application use case

In this case, the primary actor is the loan officer, whereas the secondary actor is credit rating application, which is assisting the loan officer in completing the "review loan application" use case.

USE CASE RELATIONSHIPS

Use cases represent functionalities of a system, so they may have relationship with other use cases in the system. In this section, we are going to look at these relationships.

Include

Include relationship between use cases indicate a special association. It's used to separate out common use cases so that commonly used features can be grouped together. It promotes re-usability and saves development time.

Illustrated Example – Include Relationship

Consider the simple requirement for ATM machine software. Typical functionalities of an ATM software are as follows:

- Check Balance
- Withdraw Money
- Transfer funds
- Authentication with PIN

On closer analysis, we realize that a bank customer must enter the PIN and the card, before making any transaction. That means Authentication functionality is common to all the transactions. This relationship is shown as <<include>> relationship. The use case model is as shown below:

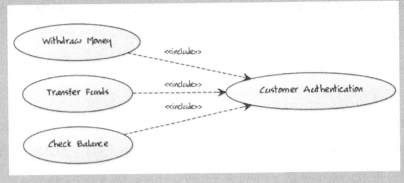

Fig 5.4 Use with Include

As you can see, we have a common use case "Customer authentication" in the above diagram.

What is << >> in <<include>>. << >> is known as stereotype in UML notations. It indicates a type of association.

Extend

Extend is used to present a specialized case for a use case. It is used to indicate either a special case for a use case or an error condition for a use case.

If a software system is not working and the customer must be shown a nice message like

Oops, something went wrong, try after some time

This functionality of showing error message is shown as an <<extend>> relationship, wherever applicable.

Illustrated Example – Extend Relationship

In a banking system, when a customer opens an account, a process is followed to open the account for the customer. Every customer gets some privileges as a customer of the bank. However, some of the customers are given "HNI status", which makes them eligible for higher interest rates and many other privileges. So, opening HNI account is a specialized case for "Open bank account", as shown in the diagram below:

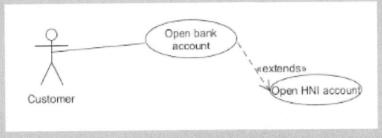

Fig 5.5 Extend relationship in Use case

SYSTEM BOUNDARY

Another important aspect of making use case model is to indicate the system boundary. System boundary is a rectangular box which is used to indicate the system boundary, used specially for use case model.

Illustrated Example – Use Case model with system Boundary

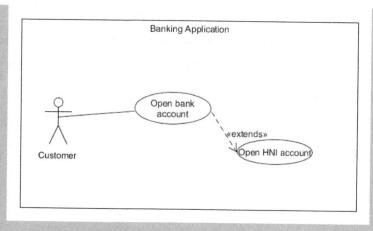

Fig 5.6 System Boundary

HIERARCHY OF ACTORS

Actors can also have relationship amongst them. One of the most common relationships is the parent-child relationship. Known as "Inheritance" in object oriented terminologies, it refers to the fact that one actor possesses all the features of parent actor but also has its additional features.

A real world example is of Dog. A Labrador variety of dog has all the features of a common dog but is different from an Alsatian variety of dog. In this case, both Labrador and Alsatian have all the features of a dog (four legs, can run etc) but also have their specific features. This is known as inheritance.

Illustrated Example – Inheritance

In a banking system, an HNI customer of a bank can be said to be inheriting from the normal customer of the bank. This relationship is shown below:

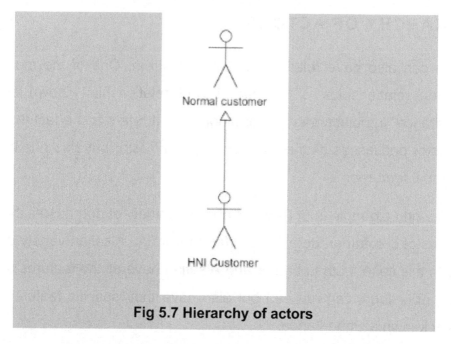

Fig 5.7 Hierarchy of actors

CASE STUDY: MOBILE BANKING SYSTEM

This case study was initiated in the previous chapter and has been re-produced for reference purpose only.

Mobile Banking System

A new age bank Incarta Development bank is planning to launch its mobile banking app. The bank plans to provide following banking operations on the mobile app with adequate level of security.

The bank is intending to allow its customers to use features related to the following divisions:

- Retail Banking
- Home Loans
- Credit Cards
- Mutual Funs

The services, which the bank is planning to offer to its customers are as shown below:

- View Bank Balance
- Transfer Funds
- Pay Credit Card Bill payment
- View Bills
- View Transactions

The bank is based in multiple cities across India.

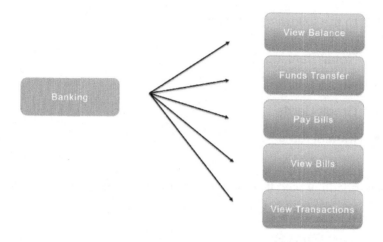

Fig 5.8 Structural view of Mobile banking system

How do we go about creating the use case model for this system?

First step is to identify the actors in the system, who are the actors in this case. One obvious actor is the **bank customer**. Do we have another one? At this point, some of you might not be able to identify another one, so let it get evolved?

The next step is to identify the use cases. The system model and the requirements indicate the use cases and they are:

- View Bank Balance
- Transfer Funds
- Pay Credit Card Bill payment
- View Bills

- View Transactions

This is a good starting point to create the first use case model as shown below:

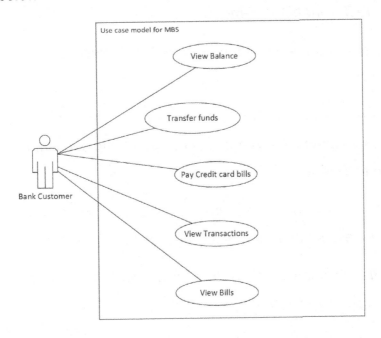

Fig 5.9 use case model for mobile banking system

At this point, a business analyst should strive to get into the details, if all the use cases have been identified? Asking open ended questions is extremely helpful.

Some of the open ended questions, you may ask at this stage are:

- *How does funds transfer take place? Tell me the steps involved?*

- *What is the process of credit card bill payment? Will the customer be seeing the bills automatically?*

- *What's the meaning of transactions? Is it bank statement or credit card bill statement?*

Considering the first question, here is the answer received from the customer:

Funds transfer can be done to any account in India by adding the beneficiary as a payee. A beneficiary means the account holder, who is going to receive the funds.

Further questioning and discussions on these requirements leads to the more detailed answers as shown below:

Funds transfer can be done to own account in the bank or to any other account holder of the same bank.

Transfer can also be done to any other account of any bank in India. This transfer happens through NEFT or RTGS.

RTGS allows to transfer funds worth 2 lakhs and above while NEFT allows the transfer below 2 lakhs.

NEFT and RTGS allow transfer in defined business hours only.

There is another payment method called IMPS, which allows 24X7 funds transfer.

The new terms during requirements discussion should raise more questions. This time you need to understand what are these funds transfer methods? Does it happen within the bank or outside the bank? Who manages these system?

This round of discussion leads to discovery of one or more external system as shown below:

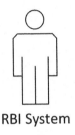

RBI System

Fig 5.10 Actor for MBS

We can name it as *RBI system* or *External funds transfer system*.

This will lead to modification in the use case model as shown below:

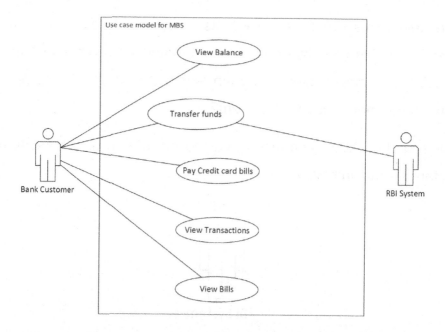

Fig 5.11 Use case model II for MBS

As discussed earlier, requirements gathering is an evolutionary technique. The requirements evolve as we continue the process of modelling and confirmation.

Extending the funds transfer use case, the customer reveals more details about this use case:

Funds can be transferred to own account (if the customer has another account).

*Funds can also be transferred to an account holder in the same bank. In that case, the account holder (the beneficiary) has to be added in the system as a **payee**.*

*Funds can also be transferred to an account holder in another bank. In that case, the account holder (the beneficiary) has to be added in the system as a **payee**. The mode of transfer could be NEFT, RTGS and IMPS. NEFT and RTGS have a defined business hour whereas IMPS can be done 24X7.*

At this stage, we can clearly observe two important info:

a) Transfer funds actually are four different use cases, each one having different steps

b) Add payee is a common piece in every use case except – transfer to another account of the same customer.

Let's update our use case diagram:

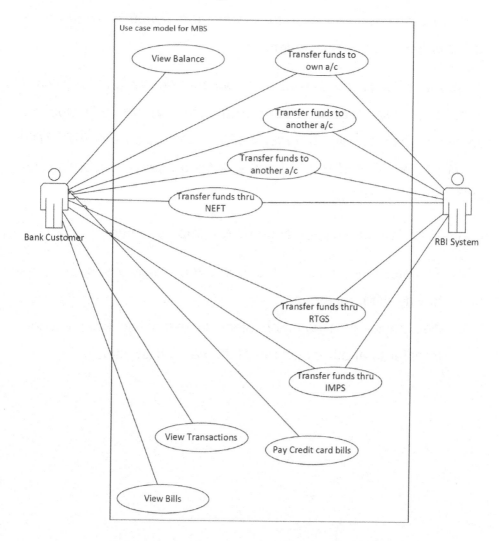

Fig 5.12 Use case model for MBS

We are almost done with the use case model. We discussed about a common function in transfer funds cases – *Add Payee.* It is being used 4 of the 5 use cases so this will be added as an <<include>> relationship.

Add payee use case will be having an <<include>> relationship with the four use cases. The final use case model will be as shown below:

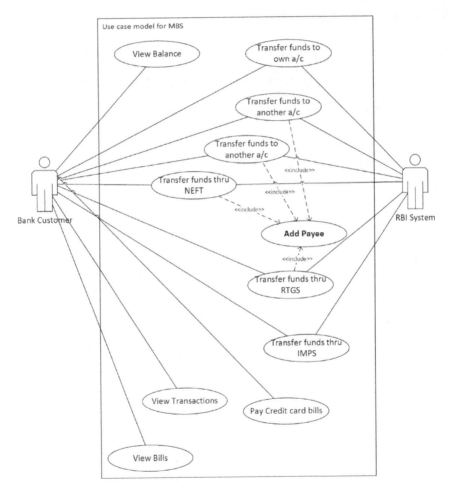

Fig 5.13 Final Use case Model – Mobile Banking System

We have created a reasonably detailed use case model for mobile banking system. There is still possibility of adding more use cases.

However, you must resist from getting the perfect use case in place as it can make the model visually complex and will defeat the purpose of being high-level.

In the next chapter, we are going to create activity diagrams based on scenarios. Activity diagrams and scenarios development phase is also known as process mapping.

SUMMARY

Use cases are simple yet most effective diagrams to capture the high level features/functions of the system. They provide an effective tool to start engaging customer stakeholders in requirements elicitation activity.

Use case diagrams comprise of actors, use cases and the system boundary. Actors are the external entities who interact with the proposed system. The use cases are representations of the way an actor interacts with the system. Use cases as well as actors have relationships.

Use case diagrams are central to all the other UML diagrams in the software development life cycle, not limited to requirements development phase.

We have discussed a full-blown case study to understand the use case modelling in this chapter. The case study is related to mobile banking.

CHAPTER QUIZ

(Choose the right option, only one option is correct)

What does an include relationship indicate in a use case diagram?

1. It shows that two use cases are having parent-child relationship?
2. It shows special conditional relationship between use cases
3. It shows the dependency relationship between use cases
4. None of these

The user of the phone should be able to make and receive calls on the phone. The phone can also remember certain numbers as favourite numbers. The phone can received data and messages from other users and can manage phone-book. A message sent by the user will be delivered to the recipient as soon as possible.

1. Make and receive calls
2. Remember favourite numbers
3. Manage phone book
4. Receive data and messages

Which of the following relationships represent the extension of the functionality of the use case to cover optional behaviour?

1. Include

2. Extend
3. Generalization
4. Specialization

Which one of the following is not a step of requirement Analysis and Modelling?

1. Requirements Elicitation
2. Stakeholder Analysis
3. Requirements Verification & Validation
4. Design

PRACTICE ASSIGNMENT

In a unique Mumbai restaurant, where majority of the staff is deaf and dumb, this system is proposed to be developed to assist the staff in managing the restaurant when clients are having food. Every waiter, necessarily a deaf and dumb person, has been allocated a set of tables, which in this case is 3. There is a manager, who is an expert in sign language and works as the intermediary between the client and the waiter. The waiter is assigned an iPAD to place the order for the table immediately, while understanding the order. The order when placed, raises an alert in the kitchen and is queued up. The chefs start preparing the items.

As and when, order gets ready (food is prepared based on eating order like soups are prepared first, followed by starters etc), the waiter is sent an alert on the iPAD along with the manager. The waiter rushes to the kitchen and brings the food.

The waiter can generate the bill after the client has finished their food. There can be cases, where discounts can be given to certain set of customer.

The system also keeps track of daily collections along with collections from each table and waiter. These statistics are available to the restaurant owners.

Assignment tasks

You are expected to complete the following tasks:

a) Identify all the functions/features of the system

b) Identify the use cases and actors and also the use case model

6. Activity Diagrams

INTRODUCTION

Activity diagrams are visually similar to flow charts and are used to represent/model processes for a business. UML 2.5 provides elements to create activity diagrams.

During the requirement elicitation process, we identify the scenarios, once we are done with the use case modelling (we have discussed use case modelling in the previous chapter). A scenario is a specific case for a business process. For example, in case of a login process, a successful login (with correct user id and password) is one scenario. Use of incorrect user id or password leads to failed attempt to login is another scenario, which is not successful. This is known as alternate scenario.

Each of the business process may include normal and alternate scenarios. Scenarios are identified by steps. In a business process, each of the possible scenarios will have one or more steps.

A business process diagram (like activity diagram) should have the capability to incorporate all such scenarios. UML Activity diagrams do have such capabilities.

ACTIVITY DIAGRAM ELEMENTS

Let's first have a look at the elements of an activity diagram, as per UML 2.5 specifications

Start Node

The initial state in an activity diagram is used to show the start of the activity diagram. It is represented as solid dark circle as shown below. There can only be one Initial State on a diagram.

Fig 6.1 start node

End Node

Final States of an activity diagram is used to show the end of a process. It's possible to have multiple end points for any activity diagram. The final state of an activity diagram is as shown below:

Fig 6.2 End node

Steps or activity state

Activity states mark an action by an object. The notations for these states are rounded rectangles, the same notation as found in State chart diagrams.

A state is nothing but a step in a business process.

Transition

An activity state is connected to the next element by transition arrow as shown below.

Let's try and a see how does an activity diagram look like:

Fig 6.3 Simple Activity Diagram

Decision Box

One of the most important elements for an activity diagram is the decision box. Decision boxes allow to show decision being taken in the business process. Every business process comprises of multiple steps with different execution paths based on conditions.

The decision box in the activity diagram is shown as diamond:

To understand how the decision box is used in an activity diagram, we will take a simple example.

Illustrated Example – Simple Activity Diagram

In this example, we will model a simple business process of funds transfer for a bank customer. The bank customer is looking to transfer INR 12,000/- to his/her friend's account. It's obvious that the transfer can only happen, if his/her account has more than 12,000/-. In case, the balance is insufficient, the system will throw a message.

The diagram below shows the activity diagram for this process.

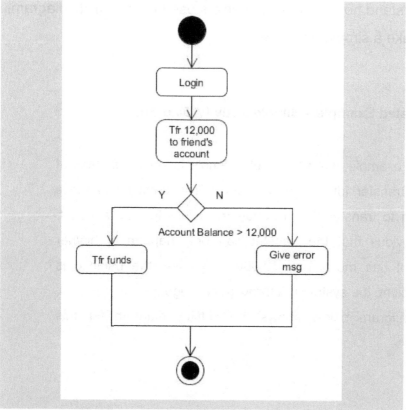

Fig 6.4 Activity diagram – Funds transfer

JOIN & FORK

Join & Fork are elements, which are used to help present the execution paths better. Fork breaks down the step into multiple parts, whereas Join allows multiple execution paths to join together.

Fork and join are not mandatory for every activity diagram. Fork is used to show execution of a process in parallel. Similarly, join is used to join multiple parallel paths to follow common execution path, there onwards.

The previous example has been redrawn using join just before the stop.

Illustrated Example – Activity diagram with JOIN

In this example, the activity diagram of previous example has been drawn using JOIN element of an activity diagram.

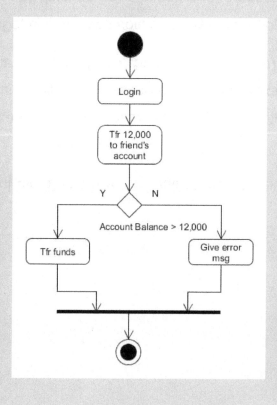

Fig 6.5 Activity Diagrams

UNDERSTANDING SCENARIOS

Scenarios play a significant role in understanding the business processes.

A scenario is

"A narrative description of what people do and experience as they try to make use of computer systems and applications"

[M. Carrol, Scenario-based Design, Wiley, 1995]

A scenario is used to capture possibilities of a business process. A business process can be multiple number of scenarios based on various conditions.

A scenario includes the following:

- Success scenario or Normal flow of events in the scenario
- Exceptions to the normal flow of events
- Information about concurrent activities
- A description of the system state at the end of the scenario

Consider the cash withdrawal process from an ATM. You need the cash urgently for some emergency reasons. What can happen at the ATM?

- It's possible that ATM is out of order
- It's possible that a refilling is underway at the ATM and you will have wait
- It's possible that the ATM does not have the currency denominations you are looking for?
- It's also possible that there is a long queue and you may have to wait for half an hour or so

What are you going to do if you encounter the possibilities mentioned above? If you assumed that you will be able to withdraw cash from the ATM without any hassles, you have a problem.

A software application should also be developed keeping in mind every possibility. We use scenarios to identify the possibilities and then decide the appropriate response in collaboration with the customer.

Let's understand the concepts with the help of an example.

Illustrated Example – Credit Card Bill Payment Scenarios

Let's consider the case study of a customer of Incarta Development bank logging into the website to pay the credit card bill.

Generally, the credit card bill is paid from the customer's bank account. In this particular case study, what are the possibilities:

- The bill is paid by the customer successfully
- The customer does not have sufficient balance
- The customer pays the min amount due because of insufficient balance

How do we create the activity diagram incorporating all the scenarios mentioned above? See the diagram to understand how scenarios are merged in an activity diagram.

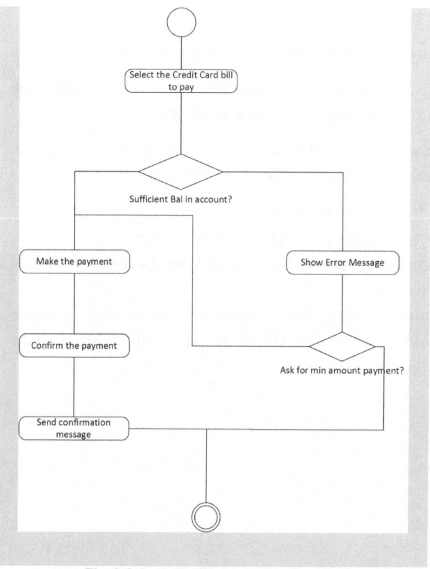

Fig 6.6 Activity Diagram for Funds Transfer

SWIM LANE

Swim lane is a strong feature of the activity diagrams as compared to flow charts. Swim lanes help in segregating the steps executed by various roles participating in a particular business process. As we have discussed earlier, activity diagrams are used to model business processes. It's possible that more than one user may participate in a business process. Swim lanes can be used to show case that. Let's take an example to show the usage of swim lanes.

Illustrated Example – Activity diagram with Swim lanes

In this example, an activity diagram is created with swim lanes. Consider a restaurant, where a customer places an order with the sales staff. The sales order passes the order (through a mobile device) to the kitchen. The kitchen delivers the order to the sales staff, who serves to the customer. Customer finishes the food and makes the payment, before leaving.

There are three actors here:

- Customer
- Sales Staff
- Kitchen

When we are creating the activity diagram with swim lanes, we provide more information for the readers. The swim lanes clearly show the actions performed by each actor in the overall process.

You can see it in the activity diagram:

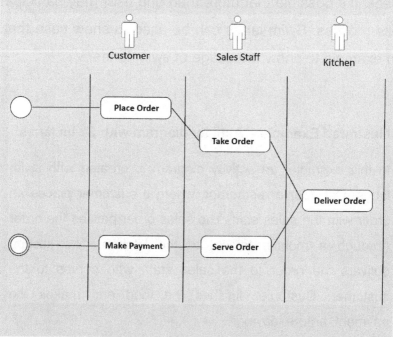

Fig 6.7 Activity diagram with Swim Lanes

CASE STUDY

Mobile Banking System – Activity Diagram

This case study is the extended case study used across the book. Through this case study, you will learn the complete UML modelling process ending with a specification document. We have already created the use case model for this case study.

In this chapter, we are going to show the activity diagram for one of the use cases *Funds transfer through RTGS*

Illustrated Example – Funds Transfer through RTGS

In the previous chapter, we developed the use case model for Mobile banking system. One of the use cases was Funds transfer through RTGS. In this example, we are going to create the activity diagram for this use case.

The reason for choosing to create an activity diagram is for the following reasons:

- It's a multi-step process and have multiple scenarios associated with it
- It also has a sub-process, which is not only used by this but by other use cases as well (ADD PAYEE)

As discussed earlier, it's a good practice to identify the

scenarios before we create the activity diagram. The scenarios associated with funds transfer through RTGS are as follows:

- If payee exist, then the customer proceeds to transfer funds through RTGS
- If the payee does not exist, the customer Adds the Payee and then proceeds to make payment
- If the amount to be transferred is less than 2 lakhs, the system shows an error message and exits

Each of the scenarios will have steps. For example, in case of first scenario, the steps would be as follows:

1. Customer chooses the RTGS option
2. Customer Selects the Payee, if it exists
3. The customer enters the amount and proceeds
4. The customer confirms the payment (the exact method may vary)
5. The system sends a confirmation SMS

We can identify the steps for other scenarios as well, before proceeding to make the activity diagram.

The activity diagram for the RTGS Funds transfer would be as shown in the diagram.

The activity diagram for RTGS funds transfer is as shown in the diagram.

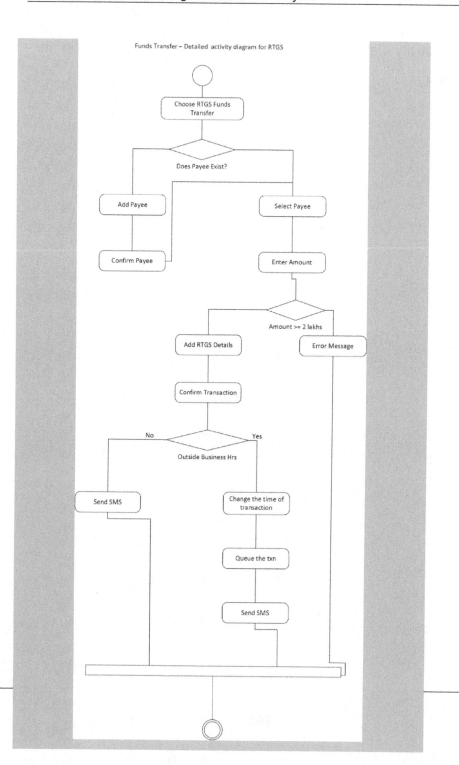

Funds Transfer – Detailed activity diagram for RTGS

Fig 6.8 Detailed RTGS funds transfer activity diagram

Having created the funds transfer activity diagram, we would be discussing the sequence diagrams in the next chapter and will create the sequence diagram for RTGS funds transfer.

CASE STUDY #2

Library Management System

Let's take a case study to demonstrate the use case modelling steps discussed so far.

A Library Management System is an automated software system in an institution.

Students and faculty are members of the library and have to be registered in the LMS system to avail the facility.

The librarian manages the offline and online system. Books are added/Edited/Deleted in the library by the librarian.

The books purchased by the librarian are of 3 types – Journals, Magazines, Study books. Each book is placed at a specified location.

Students and faculties are members of the library and they are supposed to pay a fees for getting a book from the library.

When a member requests for a book, LMS checks for its availability and if it is available, it is issued to the member.

When a book is issued, it is given for a fixed period and if there is a delay in returning the book, a fees is fined. Every member has a limit of max number of books that can be issued.

The first step is to identify the key functions of this system. The best way to identify the key functions is to identify the verbs/actions in the description. You can see that, there are following functions mentioned in the description:

- Issue a book
- Add a member
- Add/Edit/Delete a book
- Pay fees
- Request a book

Identification of functions is an iterative process, we can possibly identify more functions during further discussions with the customer.

The next step is to create the use case model for these functions. Once the use case model is created, the next step is to figure out the usage scenario for each use case (functions) listed above. In this example, let's do it for **Issue a book** function. Which are the different scenarios associated with this function?

Issue a book scenarios

- *Book is issued to a member when its available*

- *Book is not available*

- *Requesting person is not a member*

• *The member has reached the limit of books to be issued*

As you can make out, these scenarios are different situations, which arise, while issuing the book. Once we have identified the scenarios, it is expanded further to identify the steps for each of these scenarios.

Scenario 1: Success scenario

Book is issued to the requester

1. The student/faculty makes an enquiry about a book
2. The librarian checks the availability of book.
3. If the book is available, the librarian checks if the requesting member is a member of the LMS system.
4. If the requester is a member, the librarian will check the limit of books for this member.
5. If the limit is not crossed, the librarian will issue the book to the member.
6. The librarian will add the date of issue, due date and membership id of the member, to whom the book is issued.
7. The book status is updated.
8. The member record is updated.

Scenario 2: Alternate scenarios

Book is not available

In case the book is not available, the member is informed and no further action is needed.

Scenario 3: Alternate scenarios

Book is available but requester is not a member

1. In case of member not registered with the LMS, the librarian will ask for required details and identification
2. The librarian will add the member in the LMS system by entering member data
3. Once the registration is done, step 4 of the main flow will start.

An activity diagram models all the scenarios in a single diagram as shown below:

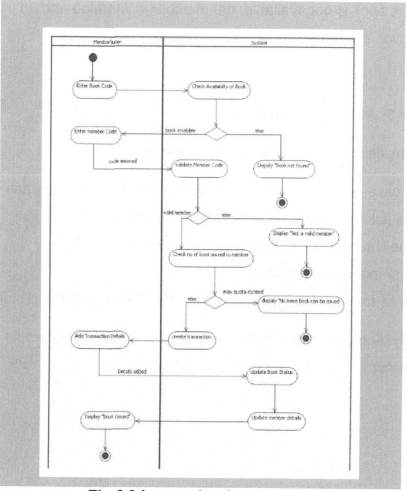

Fig 6.9 Issue a book activity diagram

SUMMARY

In this chapter, we looked at creating activity diagrams and scenarios. Scenarios are developed immediately after creating use cases. Use cases are high level system functions from user's perspective. Every use case may have multiple possibilities and each of these possibilities are known as scenarios.

Scenarios can be successful or error scenarios. It's important to identify all the scenarios related to a use case. These scenarios are not only important from system requirements completeness perspective, they are also important input for development team.

Scenarios and activity diagrams become the inputs for sequence diagrams, which is discussed in the next chapter.

CHAPTER QUIZ

(Choose the right option, only one option is correct)

What is the purpose of creating activity diagrams?

1. To demonstrate the actors and their relationship with processes
2. To demonstrate the use case relationships
3. To demonstrate the business processes
4. None of these

In many cases there is no need to create a graphical representation of a usage scenario.

1. TRUE
2. FALSE

UML activity diagrams are useful in representing what kind of system view?

1. Scenario based view
2. Behavioral View
3. Flow based View
4. None of these

ASSIGNMENT

This software system is to be designed to allow passengers to check in and get the boarding pass for flying. The baggage can also be checked-in, which is optional. The check-in can happen by the counter clerk or by the passenger using kiosk.

The system should allow individuals as well as group of passengers to check-in through the system. The boarding pass can be issued through this system. Passengers below 4 yrs need not have tickets. The airport also allows to provision for the special needs of passengers like wheelchair etc.

The system should also be able to capture the fact that the baggage for a passenger is screened by security.

Assignment Tasks

This project will be taken as a full project and will be executed end-to-end. In this chapter, you are expected to complete the following:

a) Identify all the key functions/features for this project
b) Identify and describe all the scenarios

7. Sequence Diagram

INTRODUCTION

Sequence diagrams document the interactions amongst components of a system to achieve a goal. These goals are typically the system features identified as use cases. In order to achieve the goal, the system components interact with each other and these interactions are captured in the sequence diagram. What do we mean by system components?

System components are parts of a software system (being developed) and the actors, who are working together to complete a task.

The interactions are shown as messages and these messages are shown in a sequential order (in the order in which they happen).

Every use case may have corresponding sequence diagrams. But we don't create sequence diagrams for every use case. The reasons for making a sequence diagram are:

- Use case diagram and the activity diagrams are not able to help the business process completely, it requires further understanding

- The business process does have steps which occur in a particular order

I must also highlight that creating sequence diagram is not an academic or mandatory step of requirements analysis and modelling process. It is a complex diagram to be understood by everyone and takes a lot of time to create. There has to be good reasons for creating sequence diagrams.

SEQUENCE DIAGRAM SYMBOLS

How does a sequence diagram look like? Let's first have a look at a typical sequence diagram, before we dissect it and understand the elements of a sequence diagrams.

Client places Order

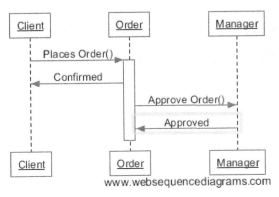

www.websequencediagrams.com

Fig 7.1 A Sequence Diagram

Let's now look at the elements of a sequence diagram:

Lifeline

The Lifeline identifies the existence of the object over time. The notation for a Lifeline is a vertical dotted line extending from an object.

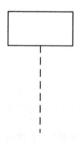

The rectangular box on the top of the image indicates the object (or a system component).

As discussed earlier, an actor can also participate in the sequence diagram and the lifeline with an actor looks as shown below:

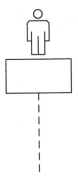

Note: We are going to use system component or object interchangeably

Activation

Activations, modeled as rectangular boxes on the lifeline, indicate when the object is performing an action or sending a message to another object. The lifeline is shown with a rectangular box on the lifeline.

The box is shown only for the duration for which the actor or the object is interacting with the other actor or object.

As you can see in the diagram below, the lifeline is shown only for the timeframe when the actor is trying to login to the system.

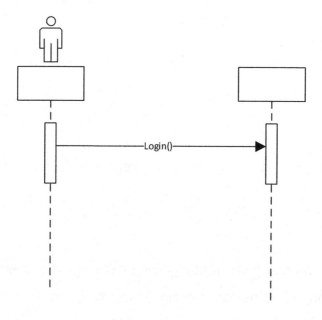

Fig 7.2 Lifeline in a sequence diagram

Message

Messages, modeled as horizontal arrows between lifelines, indicate the communications between objects or system objects.

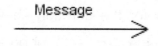

Then, we follow a simple left to right method of writing script. In the diagram titled "Lifeline in a sequence diagram", *login()* is shown as a message. Let's understand what does this message mean?

In simple terms, the user (who is an actor here) has entered the **userid** and **password** on the login screen and is clicking the **"Login"** button. This in turn sends a signal to the system (actually a system component) to check the **userid** and **password** and allow the user to login.

There is a provision to show return message or response to every communication in a sequence diagram. So, if the user is requesting for a login, then the system must also respond about the status of the request. This is referred to as a *return message* and is shown as:

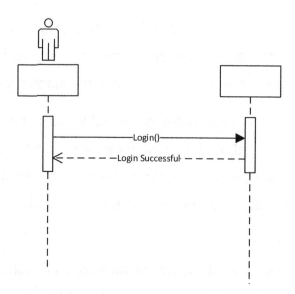

Fig 7.3 Sequence diagram with return message

The return message is shown with dotted lines as shown in the diagram above. However it may also be shown as solid line, it depends on tools. So a return message can be shown as anyone of the following:

Let's take an example to have a basic understanding of sequence diagrams.

CREATING A SEQUENCE DIAGRAM

Illustrated Example – Simple Sequence Diagram

In this example, we see a simple case of a customer/client placing an order with a supplier.

This sequence diagram has just two participating components. One is client, who is placing the order and the other one is **Order,** which is getting created. We could have used supplier/company as another object but since an Order gets created as a result, we have chosen to name this component as **Order**.

We have used www.websequencediagrams.com to create the sequence diagrams. This tool has already been discussed in the previous chapters.

In the following section, I am going to explain, how we create the sequence diagram using websequencediagrams tool. This is an online and free tool.

To create the sequence diagram as shown in the simple sequence diagram example, we have used www.websequencediagrams.com. We can also use other tools.

I like this tool as it allows me to write simple English like scripts to create the sequence diagram.

Let's look at script used for the sequence diagram in the previous example. The first line of the script is as follows:

```
1  title Client places Order
2
3  Client->Order: Places Order()
4
5
6
7
8
```

Fig 7.3 Websequencediagrams.com tool Script

In the above script, Client -> Order means that client is sending a message to Order object in the system. The message name comes in the end preceded by ':'. The message is **Places Order()**. These are free flowing texts, however care must be taken to use the same text for a particular component or message should be used everywhere.

To show the return message to the originator, we just reverse the order as shown below:

```
1  title Client places Order
2
3  Client->Order: Places Order()
4  Order->Client: Confirm Order()
5
```

Fig 7.4 Websequencediagrams.com tool Script

Result of this second line of message is as shown below:

Client places Order

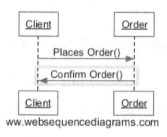

www.websequencediagrams.com

Fig 7.5 Sequence Diagram with return message

In order to show the timelines in the sequence diagram, we can use '+' and '-'symbols. Timelines show the finer detail of an object. It indicates that the object (or system component) exists during the timeline, absence of timeline means that it does not exist or not communicating.

```
1   title Client places Order
2
3   Client->+Order: Places Order()
4   Order->-Client: Confirm Order()
5
6
7
```

Fig 7.6 Script for sequence diagram

As you can see, in the diagram above, we have used a '+' sign before Order object. Usage of this sign means start of the timeline. To end the timeline, we can use '-' sign as shown in the line number 4 in the above diagram. This script generates the following diagram:

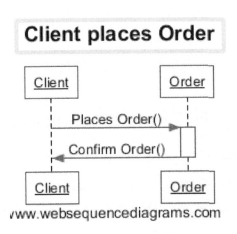

Fig 7.7 Websequencediagrams.com sequence diagram

What if we remove the '-' sign from the return message, the resulting image is as follows:

Client places Order

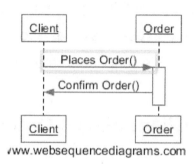

www.websequencediagrams.com

Fig 7.8 sequence diagram

In this case, the timeline does not end and continues. Now, let's add the next step in the diagram. In this case, the Order object sends a message to the Manager object for approving the order and the Manager object approved the order. The script for the same is written as follows:

```
1  title Client places Order
2
3  Client->+Order: Places Order()
4  Order->Client: Confirmed
5  Order->Manager: Approve Order()
6  Manager-> Order: Approved
7
8
9
```

Fig 7.9 Script for place an order

And the diagram will be represented as below:

Client places Order

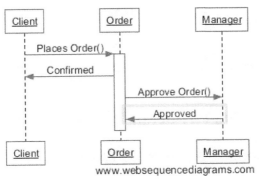

www.websequencediagrams.com

Fig 7.10 Sequence diagram for place an order

So, now we have created a simple sequence diagram which shows the following steps:

a. The client places an order, which the Order object asks to confirm, which is then confirmed by the client.

b. The Order object, then sends the message to the Manager for approving the order, which he/she does

However, we need to add the last return message to the Client object with confirmation that the order has been placed.

```
1  title Client places Order
2
3  Client->+Order: Places Order()
4  Order->Client: Confirmed
5
6  Order->Manager: Approve Order()
7  Manager-> Order: Approved
8
9  Order->Client: Order placed
10
```

Fig 7.11 Script for place an order

Now, our sequence diagram looks like this:

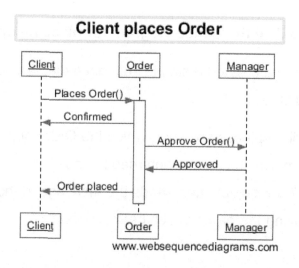

Fig 7.11 Sequence diagram for place an order

CONDITIONS IN SEQUENCE DIAGRAM

As you can make out from the above flow, there is something odd about every order going to the manager for seeking approval. That does not happen in real practice. In real practice, there could be a different scenarios for the same. Let's consider that scenario:

- If the order value is less than or equal to 10,000 then no approval is needed
- If the order value is more than 10,000 and the less than or equal to 50,000, then the Manager has to approve the order
- If the order value is more than 50,000 then the Chief manager has to approve

These three conditions are necessary to be checked before placing the order. To show the IF and ELSE condition in sequence diagram, we use ALT object as shown below:

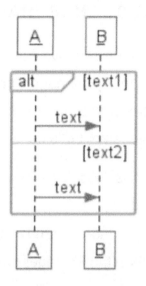

Fig 7.12 Conditions in Sequence diagram

The ALT object automatically generates a script as below, ALT represents IF and ELSE execution block. We can add multiple ELSE in this ALT statement group:

```
 1    title Authentication Sequence
 2
 3
 4
 5    alt text1
 6        A->B: text
 7    else text2
 8        A->B: text
 9    end
10
11
```

Fig 7.13 Conditions in Sequence diagram

It also shows a default corresponding diagram for the above block, which keeps on changing based on the changes in the text.

Now, let's go ahead and add the conditions as per our requirements. The modified script will look like:

```
1    title Client places Order
2
3    Client->+Order: Places Order()
4    Order->Client: Confirm Order()
5
6    alt Ordervalue <=10,000
7
8    else 10,000 < Ordervalue <=50,000
9        Order->Manager: ApproveOrder()
10       Manager->Order: Approved
11   else OrderValue > 50,000
12       Order-> ChiefManager: ApproveOrder()
13       ChiefManager->Order: Approved
14   end
15
16   Order->Client: Order placed
17
```

Fig 7.14 Place an order script with conditions

Let's understand the script for creating the sequence diagram.

Alt Ordervalue <= 10,000

This line of script is similar to writing the following:

If (OrderValue <= 10,000)

The next step to create the block for other scenarios:

Else 10,000 < Ordervalue <=50,000

   Order->Manager: ApproveOrder()

   Manager->Order: Approved

This block means that if the ordervalue is between 10,000 and 50,000, then the Order will be forwarded to the manager for approval.

The manager approves the order and the status returned is "Approved".

The last part of the script is:

Else Ordervalue > 50,000

   Order->Chief Manager: ApproveOrder()

   Chief Manager ->Order: Approved

This block means that if the ordervalue is above 50,000, then the Order will be forwarded to the chief manager for approval.

The chief manager approves the order and the status returned is "Approved".

The final sequence diagram looks like:

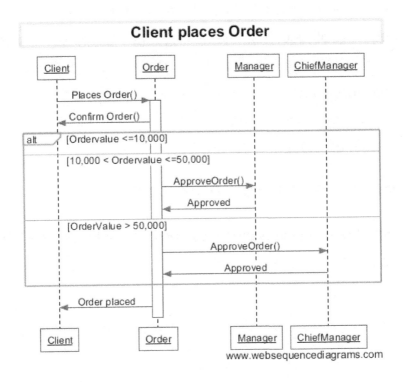

Fig 7.15 Final Sequence diagram

To summarize, the sequence diagram above, represents the following flow:

a. The client places and order, which the Order object asks to confirm, which is then confirmed by the client.

b. If the order value is less than or equal to 10,000 then no approval is needed

c. If the order value is more than 10,000 and the less than or equal to 50,000, then the Manager has to approve the order

d. If the order value is more than 50,000 then the Chief manager has to approve

e. Once the approval happens, the Client gets a confirmation message that the order has been placed

LOOPS IN SEQUENCE DIAGRAM

If some part of a business process to be demonstrated as a loop, it can also be shown as shown below:

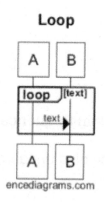

Fig 7.16 Loop in a sequence diagram

Let's take another example. With this example, we will see how to model loop in a sequence diagram. If an action has to happen multiple times, how can it be represented?

Illustrated Example – Sequence Diagram with Loop

E-commerce make a payment sequence

This business process is from an e-commerce portal. Once the client is on the website, he/she may select one or more than one items and then takes the following steps:

- The client checks out all the items from the cart
- The card adds all the items to produce the order book with total amount payable by the client (LOOP)
- The client then makes the payment using a payment gateway. In case the payment is successful, the client is informed accordingly.
- If the payment is successful, the system also checks with the client, if they need the articles to be sent by Insured Courier, if the client agrees to that, the dispatch department is also informed of the same. (OPTIONAL)

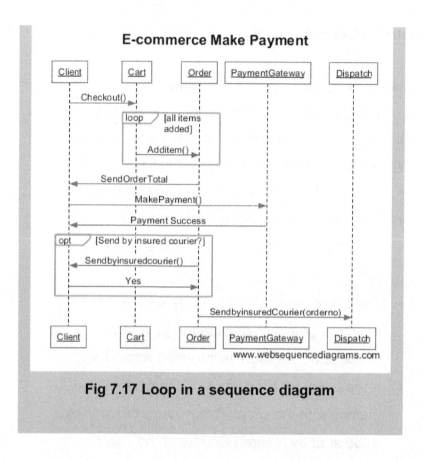

Fig 7.17 Loop in a sequence diagram

The last statement in the scenario is an optional step and sequence diagram has a specific branch for the same identified as OPT. Structure of an OPT block is as shown below:

Optional

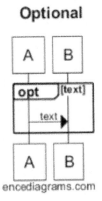

encediagrams.com

Fig 7.18 Optional Block in Sequence Diagram

The optional block is only used under specific scenario and that's why it is named as OPT.

The script for the above diagram is also shown below:

```
1   title E-commerce Make Payment
2   Client->Cart: Checkout()
3
4   loop all items added
5       Cart->Order: Additem()
6   end
7   Order->Client: SendOrderTotal
8   Client->PaymentGateway: MakePayment()
9   PaymentGateway->Client: Payment Success
10
11
12  opt Send by insured courier?
13      Order->Client: Sendbyinsuredcourier()
14      Client->Order: Yes
15  end
16
17  Order->Dispatch: SendbyinsuredCourier(orderno)
18
```

Fig 7.19 Script for Optional Block

The same exercise can be done in UMLet tool, which we have used for drawing use case and activity diagrams. Let's see, how it looks in UMLet:

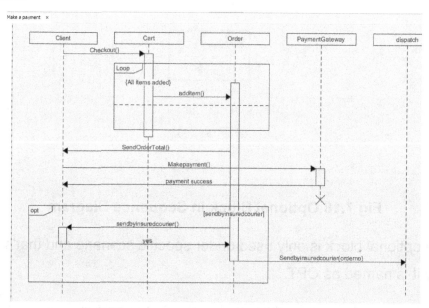

Fig 7.20 Sequence Diagram using UMLet

In UMLet also, we need to write the script, it is little more complex than Web sequence diagrams tool. However, with just a little bit of effort, you can manage that.

Start by selecting the "UML Sequence – All in One" from the right top corner drop down. This will provide you two options of combined sequence diagrams, select the second one.

Then modify the original script to create the sequence diagram as above. The script is shown below:

```
Properties
title=Make a payment
obj=Client~a
obj=Cart~b
obj=Order~c
obj=PaymentGateway~d
obj=dispatch~f

a->>>b : Checkout(); on=b
combinedFragment=Loop~bc b c;
b:{All items added}; on=c
b->>>c:additem();
..=bc;
--;
off=b
c->>>a:SendOrderTotal();
a->>>d:Makepayment();on=d
d->>>a:payment success;off=d
destroy=d;
combinedFragment=opt~opt1 a c; c:[sendbyinsuredcourie
c->>>a:sendbyinsuredcourier();on=a
a->>>c:yes;off=a
c->>>f:Sendbyinsuredcourier(orderno);off=c
--;
```

Fig 7.21 Script in UMLet

CASE STUDY

Mobile Banking System – Sequence Diagrams

This case study is the extended case study used across the book. Through this case study, you will learn the complete UML modelling process ending with a specification document. We have already created the use case model and the activity diagram for this case study.

In this chapter, we are going to create the sequence diagram for **Funds Transfer through RTGS.**

> **Illustrated Example – Funds Transfer through RTGS**
>
> In the previous chapter, we developed the activity diagram for Funds transfer through RTGS. The next step is to create the sequence diagram for the same.
>
> Let's have a relook at the scenarios associated with funds transfer through RTGS are as follows:
>
> - If payee exist, then the customer proceeds to transfer funds through RTGS
> - If the payee does not exist, the customer Adds the Payee and then proceeds to make payment
> - If the amount to be transferred is less than 2 lakhs, the

system shows an error message and exits

For creating the sequence diagram, we need to identify the system components or objects, which are participating in these scenarios. Which are these? Once we start identifying, we will realize that a lot of information was not captured during the creation of scenarios.

- The *customer* is the obvious component (An Actor)
- The next one is the *RTGS system* (an external actor), which is going to facilitate the transfer
- The RTGS transfer related data will be saved in *RTGS transaction* (You can name it differently as long as it sounds meaningful)
- The *Payee data* is another component, which stores the Payee data
- We also need to debit the *customer account*
- Once the transaction is successful, an SMS needs to be sent, let's call that component as *SMS module.*

Now, let's start writing the script in www.websequencediagrams.com.

Step 1: The *customer* selects the payee to transfer the money. The selection will happen from *Payee data.*

Step 2: If the payee does not exist, then the customer has to add the payee, so it is an optional step

For the first two steps, the script is as follows:

title Funds Transfer through RTGS

Customer -> PayeeData : Select Payee

opt Payee does not exist
   Customer->PayeeData: Add Payee
end

The sequence diagram at this stage looks like:

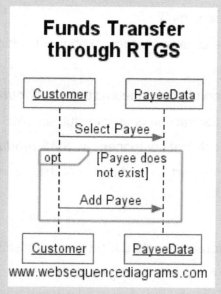

Step 3: Enter the RTGS transaction details (At this stage, you

must ask the customer, what does RTGS transaction require from the customer)? This data will be sent to **RTGS transaction**

Step 4: In case the amount is less than 2 lakhs, the system will not accept it and the RTGS transaction will throw an error. Since this is a condition, so we will be using an ALT block

The script at this stage looks as follows:

title Funds Transfer through RTGS

Customer -> +PayeeData : Select Payee

opt Payee does not exist
*   Customer->PayeeData: Add Payee*
end

Customer -> +RTGS Transaction : Enter RTGS details

alt Tfr Amount < 2,00,000
*   RTGS Transaction->Customer : Invalid Txn Amount*
else
*   Customer ->RTGS Transaction: Confirm Tfr*
end

Step 5: Once the *customer* confirms the transaction, the transaction is passed on to the *RTGS system*

Step 6: Once the transaction is completed, *RTGS system* confirms the same to *RTGS transaction*

Step 7: *RTGS transaction* also confirms the transaction with the *SMS module*.

Step 8: Finally *SMS module* sends an SMS to the *customer*

The final sequence diagram looks like

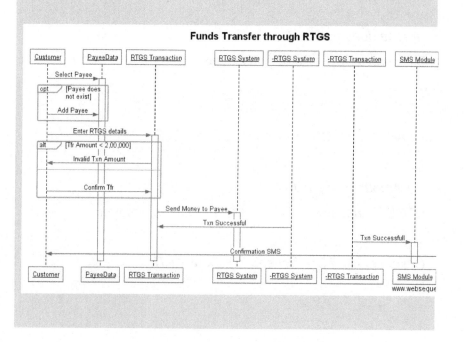

And the script for the above sequence diagram is as follows:

title Funds Transfer through RTGS

Customer -> +PayeeData : Select Payee

opt Payee does not exist
   Customer->PayeeData: Add Payee
end

Customer -> +RTGS Transaction : Enter RTGS details

alt Tfr Amount < 2,00,000
   RTGS Transaction->Customer : Invalid Txn Amount
else
   Customer ->RTGS Transaction: Confirm Tfr
end

RTGS Transaction -> +RTGS System: Send Money to Payee

-RTGS System -> RTGS Transaction : Txn Successful

-RTGS Transaction -> +SMS Module : Txn Successfull

-SMS Module -> Customer : Confirmation SMS

Please note that, creating prototypes is an essential part of every requirements analysis and modelling process. We have discussed the basics of prototyping in chapter 1.

Let's create screens for the funds transfer through RTGS use case to help customer understand the look and feel of the system as well as the look and feel of the system. We will do this in the next section.

CREATING PROTOTYPES

I have discussed prototypes, prototyping model and types of prototypes in chapter 1. One of the simplest tools for prototyping is **Pencil.** The prototype for the mobile banking system were created using pencil only.

Funds transfer through RTGS use case has been chosen to create prototypes. Add Payee and confirm payee transactions have also been created as part of this exercise.

So far, we have created the use cases, activity diagram and sequence diagrams. The prototypes can be created at any stage depending on the complexity of the system or customer requirements. Prototypes provide the depth to the system requirements. Customer stakeholders are able to see glimpses of what they are going to get? The screens created as prototypes are used to demonstrate the system functionality to the customer and get an agreement from them.

Prototypes also help you in data modelling, which we are going to discuss in the next chapter.

Please note that mobile banking system comprises of multiple use cases and features. It's not practical to create and produce all the screens in this book. That's the reason, I have selected one important feature (use case) to explain the concepts and process.

Add Payee

Purpose of this screen is to add a payee for funds transfer.

Fig 7.22 Add Payee Screen

Confirm Payee

The payee added through the "Add Payee" screen needs to get confirmed. The confirmation is done by entering the PIN sent by the bank.

Fig 7.23 Confirm Payee Screen

Initiate RTGS Funds Transfer

The RTGS funds transfer transaction is to be used for initiating the funds transfer through RTGS.

Fig 7.24 Funds Transfer through RTGS screen

Confirm RTGS funds transfer

The funds transfer transaction needs to get confirmed by PIN.

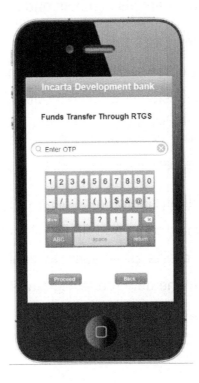

Fig 7.25 Confirm Transfer

In the next chapter, we are going to look at creation of class diagrams. Class diagrams are created to create the data model for the system.

SUMMARY

Sequence diagrams is a behavioral diagram and is used to showcase behavior of a process. In this chapter, we discussed the basics of sequence diagram, its symbols and notations.

Websequencediagrams, MS Visio and UMLet are some of the tools which can be used to draw sequence diagrams. In this chapter, we have discussed step by step creation of sequence diagrams.

Sequence diagrams are powerful diagrams. We can show conditions as well as loops in the sequence diagrams.

In the requirements analysis and modelling process, once you reach the sequence diagram stage, you will have lot of details available. At this stage, we may create prototypes to finalize the requirements details and proceed to the data modelling stage.

CHAPTER QUIZ

(Choose the right option, only one option is correct)

Which of the following diagram is time oriented?

1. Collaboration
2. Sequence
3. Activity
4. None of these

_____ are instructions sent to an object that in turn trigger methods

1. Data
2. Messages
3. Procedures
4. Attributes

A systems analyst draws a lifeline with an X at the end. This lifeline represents _____.

1. A message that cannot be delivered
2. An object that is destroyed at a point in time
3. A message that is delivered at that point in time
4. An object that is complete at that point in time

The order of messages on a sequence diagram goes from _____ to _____

1. Right to left
2. Bottom to top
3. Left to right
4. Top to bottom

8. CLASS DIAGRAMS & DATA MODELLING

INTRODUCTION

Class diagram is a structural diagram and helps in creating data model of the system. A class is a conceptual element, which is implemented later by the development team by writing code of the same.

Class is not to be confused with a table. A table is a physical representation of data structure, whereas class is a conceptual representation. A class can be implemented by one or more tables at the time of system design.

WHAT IS A DATA MODEL?

A data model presents the structure and the relationships of the data (or information). Logically and structurally related data sets are identified for the entire system by the business analysts. A data model is a visual representation of the model.

Two prominent data modelling techniques are as follows:

- E-R (Entity Relationship) diagrams
- Class Diagrams

It is possible to represent data model without using any of the techniques above. I will discuss that structure at the end of the chapter.

The primary focus of this chapter is to understand the class diagrams and how do we use it to create the data model.

WHAT IS A CLASS?

Class is a set or category of things having some property or attribute in common and differentiated from others by kind, type, or quality.

The literal definition refers class as a type, which represents related and common properties. However, we need to extend this definition for our purposes and the modified definition looks as follows:

Class is a set or category of things having common property/attribute and behavior and are differentiated from others by kind, type, or quality.

Think of a Dog as a class. All dogs, whether white or black, Labrador or German shepherd represent a creature having certain common properties and behavior. Barking, running etc represent behavior. Behavior is also referred as methods.

In software world, visitor to a website is a class, which has certain properties like name, emailID, contact number etc. A visitor also has certain behavior like searching for a product, making a purchase etc.

In the next section, we are going to understand the UML specifications for a class diagram.

CLASS DIAGRAM SYMBOLS

UML 2.5 notations for class diagram is as shown below:

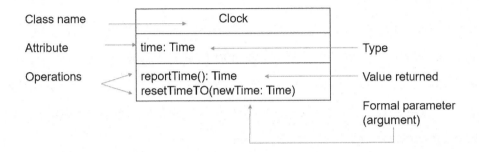

Fig 8.1 Class Diagram

Top of the diagram should include the name of the class. In this case, the name of the class is "Clock". The next section of the class diagram shows the attributes of the class. The attributes are nothing but properties or characteristics of a class. Like food can have a property as "freshness", signifying the freshness of the food. In our example, "Time" is an attribute of the clock as this is what clocks are meant for. We could also have other attributes like:

- Shape
- Number of hands
- Type (Digital/Analog)

The last section shows the methods or behavior of the class. As you can see, the class shows two methods:

- reportTime()
- resetTimeTO()

As you can make out, these are two ways in which we can interact with the clock – for getting the time and resetting the time. So as you can make out, methods represent the ways in which we can interact with a class – either for storing information, asking for information or even for processing some information.

Illustrated Example – Class Diagram

Let's take an example of a class – bank account. A bank account is owned by a customer of a bank. So naturally one of the characteristics or attributes of the account is the customer ID. In addition to that there will some other characteristics as mentioned below:

- Account number
- Type of account (Savings/Current)
- Current Balance

This can be represented as shown below:

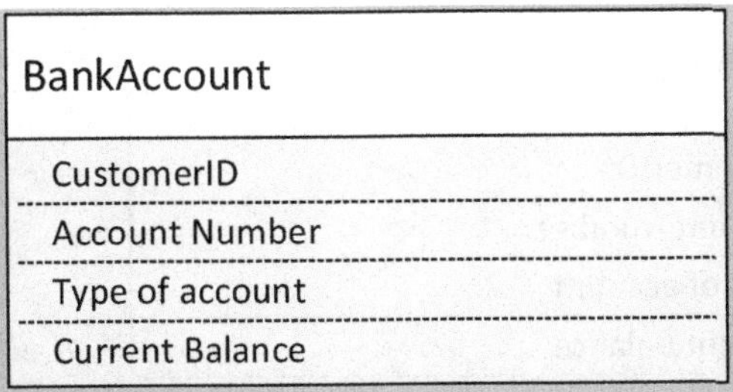

BankAccount
CustomerID
Account Number
Type of account
Current Balance

Fig 8.2 bank Account class

As you can see we have only added the properties for the class. This class diagram is incomplete as we have not yet added the behavior (methods) to it. Let's add the methods to it now. So what do you do with your bank account:

- Check balance
- Get statement

Of course, there could be more methods but we will restrict ourselves to these two. Now, our final class diagram will be as shown below:

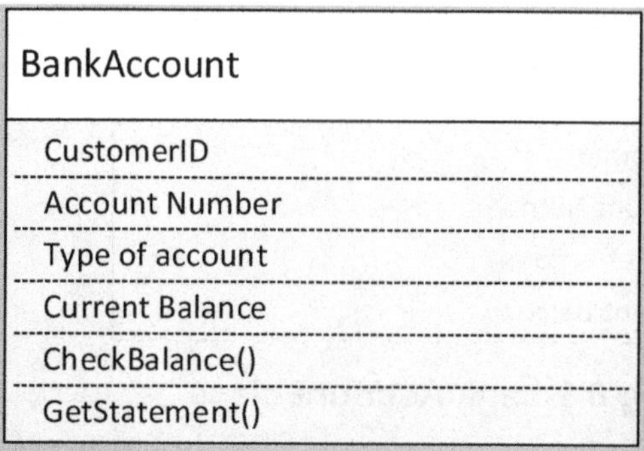

BankAccount
CustomerID
Account Number
Type of account
Current Balance
CheckBalance()
GetStatement()

Fig 8.3 Bank account class with methods

Please note the use of () as suffix to the methods. It's a convention to indicate methods or behaviors with () as suffix.

It is important to note that classes can't exist in isolation for any system. That means that there are relationships amongst the class diagrams. Class diagrams have 3 kinds of relationships as discussed below:

ASSOCIATION

Association is a relationship between two classes and is the simplest form of relationship. Association means that the two classes are connected to each other for accomplishing a task. In UML diagrams, it is shown by using an arrowed straight line from one class to another indicating – how are they associated?

However arrows can be unidirectional or bidirectional. Unidirectional means that the association is only when one class is needing other one. On the other hand, bi-directional association means that both the classes need each other.

Illustrated Example – Association in Classes

We will take a simple example where we have two classes namely homebuyer and home. A home buyer can buy one or more homes and it's a one-directional association as shown below:

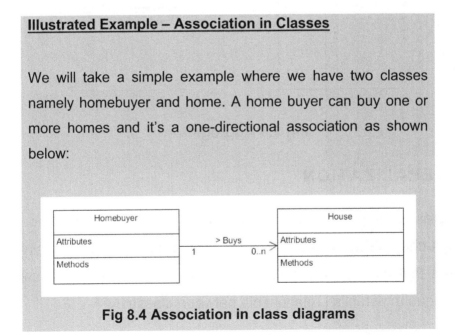

Fig 8.4 Association in class diagrams

0..n on the house side indicates that the home buyer may buy no house or any number of houses.

AGGREGATION

It's a form of an association in which one class is associated with a group. For example, a menu item belongs to a menu, which has multiple menu items. An aggregation has a diamond end pointing to the part containing the whole. This association is shown below:

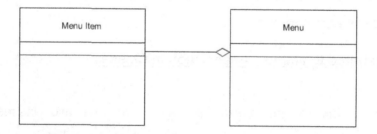

Fig 8.5 Aggregation

GENERALIZATION

Generalization is a form of association that shows inheritance or parent-child relationship between the classes. This association shows that one class is a child of other one. This is a very useful technique to establish relationship between classes.

To present an elaborate example, we have chosen this image from Wikimedia website as shown below:

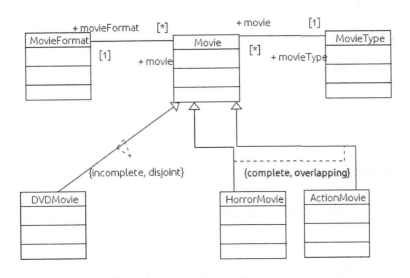

Fig 8.6 Generalization Example

In this diagram, you can see generalization amongst DVDMovie, Horror Movie and Action Movies with Movie class. Movie class is the general class from where these specialized classes of movies are created. That's the reason this relationship is referred to as generalization association.

In the above diagram, you can also see the association between Movie and the movie Type as well as between movie and movie format. There is a one to many association between movie and movie Format indicating that there can be multiple movies of a particular format. Whereas there is one-to-one relationship between movie and movie type, because each movie is of only one type. This is referred to as multiplicity.

The **multiplicity** of an association end is the number of possible instances of the class associated with a single instance of the other end.

This table gives the most common multiplicities.

Multiplicities	Meaning
0..1	zero or one instance. The notation $n..m$ indicates n to m instances.
0..* or *	no limit on the number of instances (including none).
1	exactly one instance
1..*	at least one instance

Table 8.1 Multiplicity

Every class diagram has classes, associations, and multiplicities. Navigability and roles are optional items placed in a diagram to provide clarity.

CASE STUDY

Mobile Banking System – Data Modelling

This case study is the extended case study used across the book. Through this case study, you will learn the complete UML modelling process ending with a specification document. We have already created the use case activity diagram and sequence diagrams. In this chapter, we are going to create the data model for this case study.

Let's choose the Funds transfer through RTGS process to create the data model. In the previous chapter, we created sequence diagram. When we prepare for the sequence diagram, it does provide us the foundation for creating data model.

Let's work through this case study to develop the data model using class diagrams.

> **Illustrated Example – Funds Transfer through RTGS**
>
> In the previous chapter, we developed the sequence diagram for Funds transfer through RTGS. The following steps were identified along with the system components for the sequence diagram. These components provide us the foundation for

developing the data model.

- The **customer** is the obvious component (An Actor)
- The next one is the **RTGS system** (an external actor), which is going to facilitate the transfer
- The RTGS transfer related data will be saved in **RTGS transaction** (You can name it differently as long as it sounds meaningful)
- The **Payee data** is another component, which stores the Payee data
- We also need to debit the **customer account**
- Once the transaction is successful, an SMS needs to be sent, let's call that component as **SMS module.**

The system components considered above are:

- Customer
- RTGS System
- RTGS Transaction
- Payee Data
- Customer Account

All of these are system components which are used for in the funds transfer through RTGS and are prime candidates of being classes. Only exception to this case is RTGS system. As this is an external system and is not going to be managed by our system, it is excluded as a class.

The next step is to identify the properties and behavior of these classes. We have already created prototype screens in the previous chapter, they provide lot of information about the properties of the classes. In our case, we have screens associated with:

- Payee
- RTGS Transaction

For Customer and customer account classes, customer interview, document observation or C-R-C (class responsibility & Collaboration methodology).

In this case, as customer and account are very common structures for a bank, we can ask about *the new account creation form*. This form should have complete details about customer as well as bank account.

The next step is to figure out their behavior. This can be done by asking the following questions:

- What does (this class) do or how does it work with other classes?
- How other classes interact with this class?

Let's try this for Customer class:

- Customer opens an account.
- Customer adds a payee
- Customer confirms a payee
- Customer transfer funds from their account (this also tells that customer class interacts with bank account also)

The customer class should look like this:

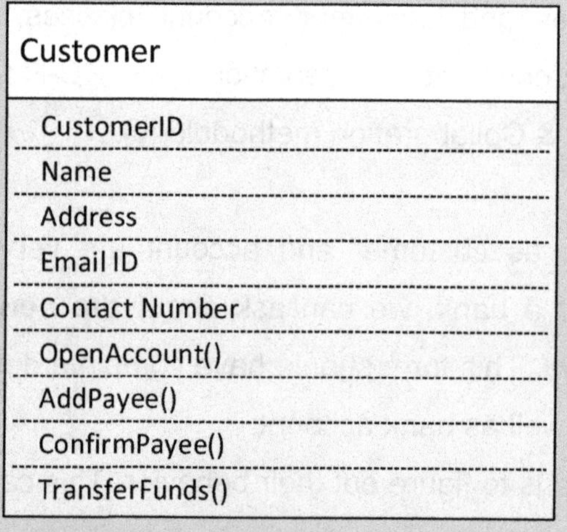

Customer
CustomerID
Name
Address
Email ID
Contact Number
OpenAccount()
AddPayee()
ConfirmPayee()
TransferFunds()

Fig 8.7 Customer class

The RTGS transaction class will have the following properties:

- Payee ID

- Customer ID
- Account ID
- Amount
- Remarks
- Priority
- Purpose

RTGS Transaction
Payee ID
Customer ID
Account ID
Amount
Remarks
Priority
Purpose

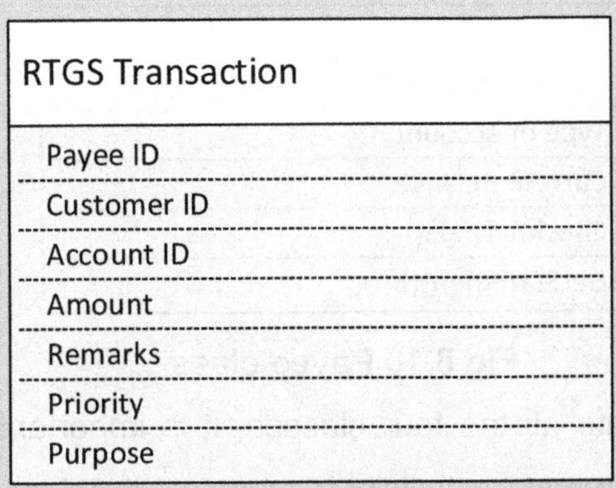

Fig 8.8 RTGS Transaction class

The next class is the Payee class and it's as shown below:

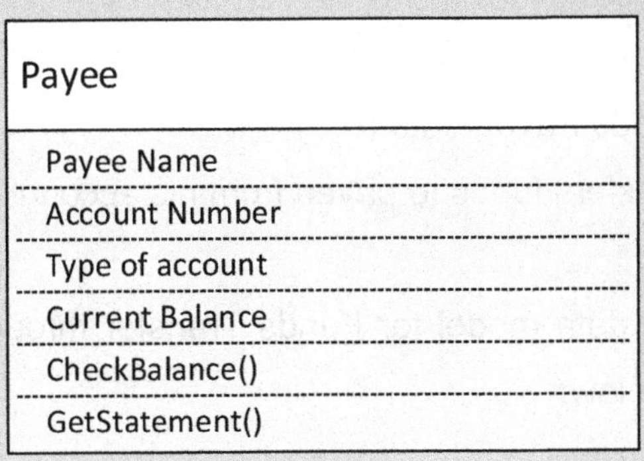

Payee
Payee Name
Account Number
Type of account
Current Balance
CheckBalance()
GetStatement()

Fig 8.9 Payee class

The customer account class, which is also part of data model for funds transfer though RTGS is as shown below:

Payee
Payee Name
Account Number
Type of account
Current Balance
CheckBalance()
GetStatement()

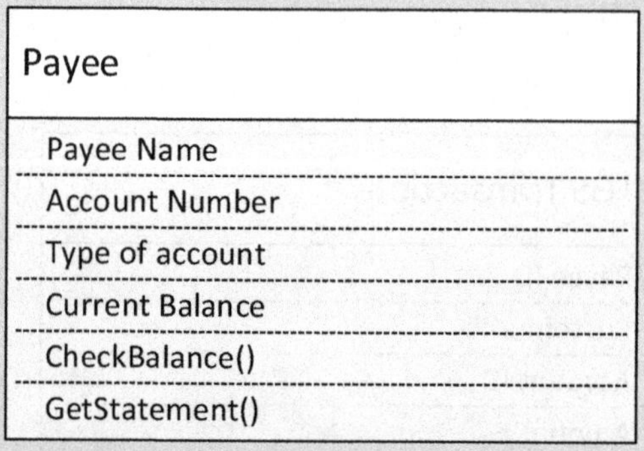

Fig 8.10 Payee class

Once we create all the four classes, it is important to show the relationship and multiplicity to complete the data model.

The relationships and multiplicity are as follows:

A customer opens account (1..*)
A customer adds Payee data (0..*)
Customer transfers funds to payee from his account (0..*)

The complete data model for Funds Transfer through RTGS is as shown below:

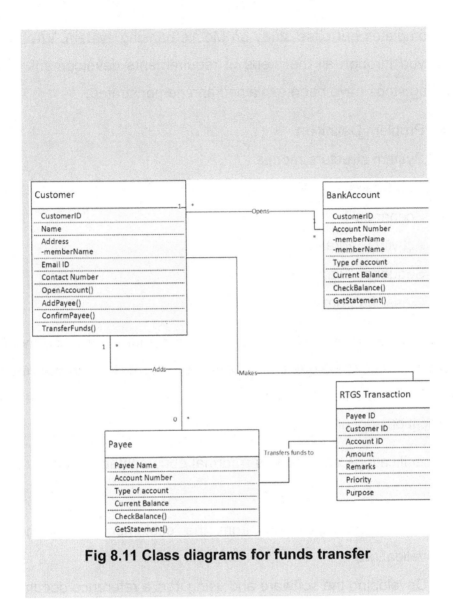

Fig 8.11 Class diagrams for funds transfer

This completes our case study on Mobile banking system. We have taken you through all the steps of requirements development. The following steps have been explained and demonstrated:

- Problem Definition
- System structure model
- Use Cases
- Scenarios
- Activity Diagrams
- Sequence Diagrams
- Class Diagrams

As a business analyst, UML modelling will comprise of these model diagrams. Once the modelling is complete, a specification document needs to be created. I am going to discuss — how to create the specifications document.

The specifications document is a formal documentation and is used for:

- Getting an agreement from the customer (Requirements validation)
- Developing the software and using it as a reference document

In sequential methodologies, we create a specification document for the entire software. However, in the iterative methodologies (like

Agile), we don't document all the requirements upfront. Instead the requirements are documented and detailed as they are taken up for development.

The UML modelling is a generic methodology and can be used in all types of methodologies. As part of business analysis planning phase, we need to decide on:

- Which diagrams need to be created?
- What kind of prototype needs to be created?
- How will we document the specifications

The factors which need to be considered to take a decision on the above:

- The timelines for the project
- The budget
- The customer's familiarity with the UML diagrams (specially sequence diagrams etc)
- Development team's familiarity with UML diagrams (specially sequence diagrams etc)

SUMMARY

Class diagrams are used to prepare the data model for a software. Class diagrams are structural diagrams and does not have any behavioral characteristics. This means that class diagrams cannot be used to model processes.

In this chapter, we discussed the symbols of class diagrams and how are they created? Class diagram is not a stand-alone diagram but they are associated with other. These relationships are described in the chapter as association, aggregation and generalization.

Creating data model for the software system is generally the last step in the requirements analysis and modelling process. Once we complete data modelling, we get into creating the specifications document.

We have discussed the requirements specifications in the next chapter.

CHAPTER QUIZ

(Choose the right option. there is only one corerct answer)

A class diagram comprises of the following:

1. Attributes and methods
2. Methods and values
3. Attributes and objects
4. None of these

Classes have relationships amongst them, choose the invalid option from the following options:

1. Association
2. Aggregation
3. Generalization

Multiplicity refers to the relationship between classes. *0..** multiplicity represents – a class may have no relationship with the other class or it may have **one to many** or **many to many** relationship. Is this TRUE or FALSE

1. TRUE
2. FALSE

The relationships shown in a data model must be classified to show their

1. Modality
2. Cardinality
3. Association
4. Both A and B

9. Requirement Specifications & Validation

INTRODUCTION

The final steps of the requirements analysis and modelling phase of any software development lifecycle methodology is to prepare a requirements specifications document after the requirements are verified and validated.

Requirements specification document can be a formal document or an informal document based on mutual agreement between the customer and the vendor (The IT Company).

The popular terms used for requirements specifications document are:

- System Requirements Specifications document (SRS)
- Functional Specifications document (FS)
- Use case specifications document
- User Stories and backlog

SRS and FS are used interchangeably and are probably the most used terms in the software industry. Use case specifications document is used in specific cases but mostly when we are using UML modelling techniques. User Stories and backlog documents are used in agile methodologies.

In this chapter, we are going to have a look at the use case specifications document and the System requirements specifications document. You will be able to develop the complete specifications document after finishing this chapter.

SYSTEM REQUIREMENTS SPECIFICATION

In most of the SDLC methodologies, you, as a business analyst, are expected to develop a detailed document capturing complete requirements. Purpose of this document is to create a reference point for further development and acceptance. The document, which captures the detailed requirements, is referred to as Functional Specification Document (FSD) or System Requirements specifications (SRS). We are going to refer to this document as SRS, in this book, from here onwards.

An SRS is

- A document that clearly and precisely describes, each of the essential requirements of the software and the external interfaces.

    - (functions, performance, design constraint, and quality attributes)

- Each requirement is defined in such a way that its achievement is capable of being *objectively verified* by a prescribed method; for example inspection, demonstration, analysis, or test.

So, what does a typical SRS document contain?

SRS FORMAT

System Requirements specification document is a comprehensive document and contains detailed information on various aspects of project including requirements.

Even though, the SRS formats vary across organizations, there are elements which will be common across all the formats. In this chapter, I am showcasing a format, which I found very useful, while managing my projects.

Let's look at the contents of a typical SRS document:

- **Objectives:** This section should mention the objective of creating the document along with the brief description of document contents.
- **Scope:** This section should mention the scope of the work in terms of development scope, performance scope and usability scope.
  This section should also contain any timeline constraints, if there are any.
- **Exclusions from the scope:** This section should mention everything which is not part of the scope. This is an important section. For example, in some cases, the UI design is not included in the scope of work. It may be done by the customer design team or it's already ready.

- **Outstanding issues:** During the requirement elicitation phase, you will be interacting with the customer team and all the issues will keep getting resolved. However, at the conclusion of the requirements phase and the finalization of this document, there could still be some issues, which will remain outstanding. These outstanding issues will be mentioned in this section in the following format:

Outstanding Issue	Responsibility	Expected closure date
The HINGT report format was to be finalized by the CEO and to be sent to us	Robert Vagh, IT Manager	15-Apr-16

Table 9.1 Outstanding issues in SRS

- **Assumptions and constraints:** This section should list down all the assumptions and constraints for the project.
- **Approvals:** This section should provide all the expectations of the stakeholders in terms of approvals of the various artifacts

relating to the project. The suggested format of the project is as follows:

Role	Name & Designation	Signature	Date

Table 9.2 Roles table in SRS

- **System description:** This section provides the overview of the system. This description can be provided in the form of block level diagrams or context diagrams etc. You can also include a system level flow diagram in this section.

- **Components and sub-components description:** This section should provide details of the sub-modules of the system, if applicable. So an e-commerce system might have sub-systems like user module, product module etc. You can include flow charts or activity diagram for the sub-modules.

- **Features description:** This section is possibly the longest section of the document, where each and every feature of the system will be described in details. In some cases, you might also have accompanying screens for each feature.

- **Non-functional requirements:** An important aspect of every software requirements specifications document is to capture functional as well as non-functional requirements. Non-functional requirements refer to the requirements related to look and feel, security (like https:// websites), performance (supporting millions of users) etc.

- **Acceptance Criteria:** This section should contain the acceptance criteria from customer viewpoint. Acceptance criteria must be specific and measurable so that they can fulfilled during the implementation time.

In the next section, I am going to discuss the use case specifications document format. In this chapter, we are also going to see how to write the specifications document examples using our case study.

USE CASE SPECIFICATIONS

Use case specifications is a specialized format suitable for capturing requirements generated using UML modelling process. The format of a use case specifications document is different from an SRS.

Let's look at the elements of a use case specifications document. As the name suggests, a use case specification document is written from use case perspective. The entire document is arranged on the basis of use cases. Each use case section will have the following format:

- **Name of the use case:** This section will have the name of the use case.

- **Actors:** This section identifies the key actors who are going to use this use case.

- **Brief Description:** In this section, we describe the use case. What does this use case all about? In this section, we also put the use case diagram.

- **Pre-conditions:** What are the pre-requisites for this use case to happen? In other words, if the actor has to perform this use case, does he/she need something to happen before performing this?

- **Input data:** What is the input data for this use case? In order to perform this task in the system, do we need some input data? The data set must be specified with size, description, type etc.

- **Flow of events:** This is a critical part of the use case. We describe the success and other scenarios in a step by step wise manner. We have discussed scenarios in the activity diagrams chapter. There could be more than one success and one alternative scenarios.

- **Post Conditions:** This is a condition which is expected to happen after the use case gets completed.

- **Output data:** What is the output of this use case? Does it create some data? The data set must be specified with size, description, type etc.

- **Extension Points:** This section lists the use cases which extend this use case. We have already discussed the <<extend>> relationship in the use case modelling chapter.

- **Includes:** This section lists the use cases which share an <<include>> relationships with the use case, we are describing. We have also discussed this type of relationship in the use case modelling chapter.

- **Activity Diagram:** In this section, we will have activity diagrams related to this use case and describes the business process in a step by step manner.

The use case specifications may not be suitable for all the scenarios as it does not include the screen design. However it's entirely possible to add the screen designs and make it comprehensive and complete to be used for further software development phases.
I am going to create the use case specification document for our mobile banking system case study. The specification document will be complete and comprehensive in all respects and will be apt enough to be used by the development team to take it forward.

CASE STUDY

Mobile Banking System – Use case specifications

Mobile Banking system is the primary case study, I have used in this book throughout. Now it's time to give it a final shape in the form of a use case specifications document.

A business analyst consolidates all the notes, understanding, minutes of meetings and UML models in the form of a specifications document.

Use case specifications document

Mobile Banking System

Introduction

This document is created to capture complete specifications for the Mobile banking system to be developed for Incarta development Bank. The intended audience for this specifications document is the customer stakeholders and the development team.

The document is divided into multiple sections based on the use cases identified during the requirements elicitation phase. Each of the use cases represents a proposed feature of the system.

Scope of work section describes the deliverables for the system expected by the bank. This section also has an exclusions section, which describes the work, which is not to be delivered by the development team.

Assumptions and constraints section describes the assumptions for the project based on discussions with the customer. It also specifies the constraints identified considering that this application is developed for the mobile devices.

Scope of work

The scope of work for us is to gather requirements, document it and get an agreement on the same from the stakeholders. The scope also includes designing, developing and testing the system before handling it over to the customer for UAT. During the UAT, we also need to support the stakeholders for big fixing and other support aspects.

Exclusions

The scope of work does not include hosting of the mobile application once developed. The hosting and maintenance of the mobile application will be taken care by the bank itself.

Assumptions and constraints

This section lists out the assumptions and constraints for this project.

Assumptions

The assumptions for this project are:

- The bank is going to provide us the interface details for RTGS, NEFT and other such interfaces

- The customer stakeholders will be available during the requirements gathering and UAT process as per agreed schedule so that the activities can be conducted on time

Constraints

The constraints of the system are:

- The application is being developed for mobile devices and this application will only work on smart devices with internet connectivity
- Mobile devices come in multiple form factors and capabilities. The application is only designed considering a minimum processor capability and mobile data speed. It may not work on legacy devices as well as any device which does not have the minimum capabilities.

System Use Cases

Use case: Add Payee

Actors: Bank Customer

Description: This use describes the functionality of adding a payee so that money can be transferred to this payee.

Use case diagram:

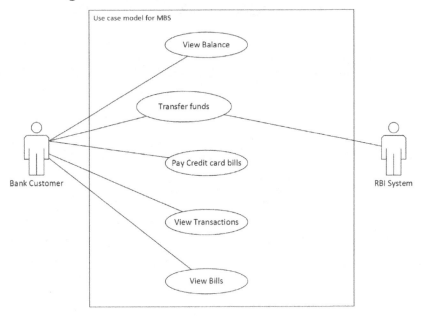

Note for readers:

I am adding the complete use case model here. Putting just one oval shape to show *add payee* is useless and does not show the context for add payee use case

Pre-conditions

The customer must be logged into the application to be able to add a payee.

Input Data

To add a payee, the customer must add the following data:

	Field name	Length	Type	Default value, if any	Field Property	Source	Remarks
1	Payee name	35	Alpha	None	Editable	Input	
2	Account Number	100	Number	None	Editable	Input	Must be a valid Email ID
3	Type of account	5	Text (ID)	None	Select	Input	Must be a drop down and will have options – Savings, Checking

4	Bank ID	20	Alpha	None	Editable	Input	Bank Code
5	Branch ID	20	Alpha	None	Editable	Input	Branch Code
6	IFSC Code	20	Alpha	None	Editable	Input	IFSC unique code
7							

Note for readers:

This table is based on your experienced as a business analyst (and confirmed with the customer) or direct questions answered by the customer. But you must have all the details as shown.

Flow of events (Scenarios)

Success Scenario: The steps for successfully adding the payee

1. The customer selects add payee link
2. Payee name is added
3. Account number is added
4. IFSC code is added directly
5. Bank Name is selected
6. Branch name is selected
7. Click on Add Payee button

8. Enter the OTP/PIN on the next screen "Confirm Payee"

Alternate Scenarios

Payee details already exist

1. The data entered by the customer already exist (bank name, account number)
2. The system throws an error stating that "The payee already exist in the system" and exits

OTP not received

1. Customer has entered all the details of the payee and has clicked on the "Add Payee" button and does not receive OTP
2. The confirm payee screen must have an option of getting the OTP again.

Post-Conditions

Once the payee is confirmed, the customer can transfer the funds to this payee.

Output Data

The status of the payee is changed after the correct OTP is entered by the customer for the new Payee.

Includes

There is no other use case, which is included by this use case.

Extends

There is no other use case, which is extended by this use case.

User Interface

The user interface for this use case is shown below:

End of Use case specification

CASE STUDY 2

Arita Nora Inc – creating SRS

Arita Nora Inc is an education provider and provides training to K12 students. It is looking to develop an online course delivery and testing platform.

The system requirements specifications document captures the requirements details for this system. The next few pages captures all the elements of a system requirements specification document.

Softedge private limited is hired by Arita Nora to develop the system.

System Requirements Specification

Learning Management System

Objectives

This document provides the detailed requirement specification of the Seminar software. The software will be developed for Arita Nora Inc. The purpose of the software is to announce the dates for a seminar as well as capture the details of the participants.

Scope

The scope of work for our company is to understand the requirements (to be documented in this document), develop and deliver the solution within the defined timelines.

Outstanding Issues

No outstanding issues.

Assumptions, Constraints and dependencies

- Arita Nora team will be available for providing us the detailed requirements
- They will also be approving/providing inputs as per the timelines to the SRS document as well as other documents where their approval is needed.

Approvals

ROLE	NAME	SIGNATURE	DATE
Client Manager	Mr. Robert Simon		
Project Director	Ms. Neha Bhasin		

Glossary

- L MS - Learning Management System
- Template – Standard formats for documents
- CR – Change Request

Component or Subsystem Description

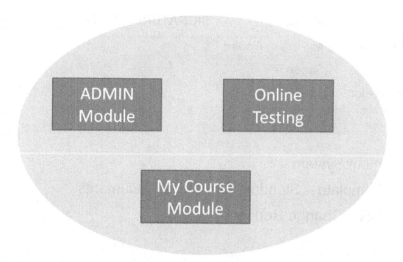

The software comprises of three basic modules:

- Admin Module
- My Course Module
- Online Testing Module

<u>Admin Module:</u> Admin module is the core module which will be used to configure and setting up the system. Admin module will have the following functions/screens:

- User Master
- Category Master
- Sub-category Master
- Question Master
- Assignment Master
- Content Master

Online Testing Module: Online testing module will provide the key functionality of choosing and appearing for a test for students who subscribe and are authorized users.

My Course Module: This module is the course delivery module, where students will be enrolling for a course and will be taking the course. Each course will have multiple modules and an assignment is to be completed after completing each module.

Features Description

This section will contain the detailed functional requirements for each module. We hace created one functionality to showcase the structure and detailing of each requirement. You are required to complete it for all the other functions as discussed.

User Master

Purpose: User master screen will be used to add a user in the system. This screen will be called from the "Masters menu" and will be listed as "User Master".

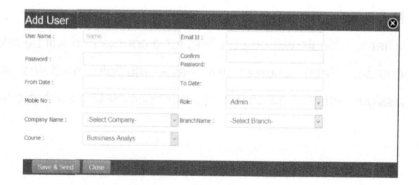

Description:

- This screen will be accessible to the system administrator only.

Data structure:

	Field name	Length	Mand-atory	Default value, if any	Field Property	Source	Remarks
1	User name	35	Y	None	Editable		
2	Email ID	100	Y	None	Editable		Must be a valid Email ID
3							
...							
..							
n							

Output/Next Step

No direct output is expected from this process, however creation/updation/deletion of a user will determine login ability of the users.

Software/Hardware Interface

No software interface identified.

Documentation

Any detailed documentation

Non-Functional Requirements

Hardware/Software Requirements

Hardware Requirements: Provide the hardware requirement along with the date

Software Requirements: provide the software requirements along with the dates.

Acceptance Criteria

All requirements implemented will be unit-tested first. A test script will be written as a guide to for testing base functional changes. This script will be used for system testing and User Acceptance Testing (UAT).

End of SRS

REQUIREMENT VERIFICATION & VALIDATION

Verification and validation are two different concepts but are used interchangeably. In this section, we are going to discuss both these concepts.

Once the requirements specifications document is prepared, the verification and validation activities are carried out. So what is verification and validation?

Requirements Verification

Purpose of requirement verification is stated below

"Ensure that requirements specifications and models meet the necessary standard of quality to allow them to be used effectively to guide further work."

Requirements verification is carried out on the requirements specification documentation. Verification activity involves checking the requirements specification document on the following parameters:

- Atomic
- Complete
- Consistent

- Concise

- Feasible

- Unambiguous

- Testable

- Prioritized

- Understandable

Atomic

An atomic requirement is independently deliverable and represents a single feature that can either be satisfied or cannot be. During the verification process of the requirements, one must look to ensure that the requirements are documented in an atomic fashion.

Requirements being atomic does not mean that every statement or sentence in a requirements specification document is atomic. Instead, it means that a particular feature of the system must be described together so that it can be understood in entirety.

Example

- A user must be able to add, edit and delete a new customer record
- As a User, I want to click a particular location from the map and thereby perform a search of landmarks associated with that latitude longitude combination.

Look at both the requirements above and determine, if they represent atomic requirements or not.

The first statement talks about **add, edit and delete** – these are independent features in themselves.

The second statement talks about search feature of a map. As it is talking about a single feature (considering map creation is part of another feature), it is an example of an atomic requirement.

Complete

The requirements must be complete, what is the meaning of completeness?

It means that all the required information to implement (*read* Code) the requirement is available. There is no need to assume anything in order to implement the same. One of the important aspects of completeness is to also have measuring units, if applicable.

Example

In case of an error, the system must exit gracefully.

I am sure, many of you must have seen this requirement before. This is an incomplete requirement, it does not provide all the information needed to implement the exit, in case of error. A complete requirement would be as follows:

In case of an error, the system must show an error page to the users with the following message:

Oops! We have encountered some error and working on it. In the while you can go to the home page and try other options or write to us about what were you doing, so that we can help. Our email id is support@abc.com

Consistent

Consistency is an important aspect of requirements. It means that all inputs to any process, must be processed similarly. It should not happen that processes produce different outputs for inputs coming from different sources. Consistent requirements also mean that you will not find a contradicting information in the SRS document.

Example

Let's look at these requirements:

Req1: *The invoices will be generated and sent automatically based on the milestones achieved with a copy to the accounts department*

Req2: *The accounts department will generate the invoice based on milestones achieved and will send it to the customer.*

The requirements mentioned above are not consistent as they are presenting contradictory information.

Concise

What does concise mean?

Each requirement must accurately describe the system in a concise manner. The requirements contains no extraneous and unnecessary content.

Example

Sometimes the user will enter Airport Code, which the system will understand, but sometimes the closest city may replace it, so the user does not need to know what the airport code is, and it will still be understood by the system.

Is this requirement concise? Not really, the concise version of the above requirement would be as follows:

The system shall identify the airport based on either an Airport Code or a City Name.

Feasible

All the requirements included in the SRS must be feasible to implement. For a requirement to be feasible, it must be:

- Implementable within the given timeframe and budget
- Implementable using the existing and chosen technology platform
- A feature, which will be used by the end users

Example

Let's look at some of the requirements below:

The developed software must be reliable and should not crash.

The developed software must be free of defects.

Both the above requirements are not feasible. There is no software which is free of defects in absolute terms.

Unambiguous

Unambiguous means a single interpretation of any sentence. If a requirement is defined in such a manner that it can only be interpreted in one way, it means that the requirement is unambiguous. All subjective words or statements must be eliminated from the requirements.

Example

Let's look at this requirement:

All the screens in the system must load quickly.

Do you think, this statement is clear? Certainly not. Nothing can be implemented from the word "quickly". It must specify clearly what the meaning of "quickly" is. A better version of this requirement would be:

All the screens in the system must load within 8 seconds.

Testable

A testable requirement can be defined as a requirement, which can be tested and validated using any of the following methods:

- Inspection
- Walkthrough
- Demonstration
- Testing

In this manner, it is possible to ensure that the requirement has been implemented correctly. Let's take an example and examine if it is testable:

The system must be user-friendly.

If this is allowed to be part of the final SRS document, how will you validate the system against this requirement, as it is not testable. So a better example would be:

The user interface should be menu driven, which will be on the top of the website along with the site index. A tool tip for all the text boxes must be provided.

Prioritized Requirements

Prioritized requirements are the requirements, which are ranked, grouped, or negotiated in terms of importance and value against all other requirements.

Prioritization helps in planning the deliver in order to provide the maximum value to the customer. If the requirements are prioritized, the development team can focus on delivering the software in phases.

The priority of the requirements can be determined based on:

- Business Value
- Risk
- Cost and benefit
- Implementation Difficulty
- Regulatory or Policy Compliance
- Relationship to Other Requirements

Understandable Requirements

Requirements should be grammatically correct and written in a consistent style. Standard conventions should be used. The word "shall" should be used instead of "will," "must," or "may." It should be represented using common terminology of the audience.

In this section, we looked at the characteristics of requirements which are used to conduct the verification of the requirements specification document.

It's possible to have an SRS document which is perfectly well documented and verified yet completely useless? Yes, that's possible.

Unfortunately, verification does not focus on checking whether the requirement is aligned with business goal or not? So we might end up with a situation, where the SRS may contain verified requirements but may end up delivering a software which is worthless for the customer.

It does not mean that requirement verification is a non-important part of SDLC, however to gain the maximum benefit, we must use validation as a complimentary process to requirements verification.

REQUIREMENTS VALIDATION

The purpose of Validate Requirements is to ensure that all requirements and designs align to the business requirements and support the delivery of needed value.

Purpose of requirements validation are as follows:

- Validation ensures that all the requirements, which are intended to be implemented are fulfilling the business needs.

- Requirements are elicited from stakeholders and only they can validate the requirements

- Requirements, which cannot be validated, should be considered to be *out of scope*

Requirements validation is a mechanism to:

- Give the customer stakeholders a chance to check early whether the proposed solution will really solve their problems

- Simulate the evolution of customers' understanding (of what is possible) and therefore act also as a catalyst of the elicitation process

So, how do conduct validation? Here are some of the techniques to perform requirements validation:

- Model-based requirements validation

    - Data-flow Modelling (DFD)

    - UML Modelling

- Prototyping

    - Throwaway Prototyping

    - Evolutionary Prototyping

- Wireframes

- Mockups

We have discussed most of these techniques in this book itself. Data flow modelling is described in Appendix section of this book. Prototyping is discussed in details in the first chapter of the book.

Requirements verification and validation is conducted in order to make sure the correct requirements are captured and documented in the correct way in the specifications document.

WHAT HAPPENS NEXT?

Once the requirements specifications are documented and approved, the document is handed over to the technology team, which starts working on the system design and coding.

The role of a business analyst is to provide clarifications to the technology team. It's possible that you as a business analyst may not have answers to all the clarifications sought. In that case, you may need to go back to the customer and get the clarifications and convey it to the team, so that they can continue their work.

Once the coding gets completed, the functional testing of the application starts. Business analysts participate in the functional testing phase before it is handed over to the customer for the user acceptance testing (UAT). A business analyst along with team members provide support to the customer for a timely completion of the UAT.

Once UAT is completed, the system will be put on production machines and actual users will start using it.

SUMMARY

Creation of requirements specifications document is the end result of the requirements development activity by a business analyst. The requirements specifications document can be a formal document or an informal document.

We have discussed two requirements specifications document formats:

- System requirements specifications (SRS)
- Use case specifications document

Functional specifications document (FSD) is another term used for requirements specifications document. The format of FSD is very similar to an SRS.

However, in agile methodologies like SCRUM, we don't create complete specifications document upfront. Instead product and sprint backlog documents are created, which essentially tabulates the user stories.

The specifications documents are verified and validated, before they are taken forward for design phase. We have discussed the verification and validation methods in this chapter.

CHAPTER QUIZ

(Choose the right option. There is only one correct answer)

Verification and Validation are not two different things but rather represent the same concept and activity

    1. TRUE

    2. FALSE

We conduct only verification on the Requirements specification document. Validation is conducted only on code

    1. TRUE

    2. FALSE

Using checklists to check the requirements document, represents which one of the following activities

    1. Verification

    2. Validation

    3. Testing

    4. None of these

Which one of the following techniques is used for validating requirements?

    1. Interviewing

    2. Prototyping

    3. Observation

    4. None of these

A major justification for an early verification activity is that many costly errors are made before coding begins.

1. TRUE   2. FALSE

PRACTICE ASSIGNMENTS

In these assignments, you are required to validate the given requirements and state what the issues with these are.

Requirement 1

The alert system, which needs to be developed, is expected to provide status messages at regular intervals, which is not less than every 60 seconds.

Requirement 2

The restaurant billing system will provide discount to the customers based on a master corporate discount list.

Requirement 3

The password should be encrypted for security reasons.

Requirement 4

The developed Software must be capable of running on any browser.

Requirement 5

The software must have a provision of maximizing the login attempts. After 3 consecutive unsuccessful login attempts, the database script must lock the user out of the system.

Appendix A: SAD

STRUCTURED ANALYSIS AND DESIGN APPROACH (SAD)

Structured analysis and design is the oldest approach to system analysis and design. In this chapter, we are going to provide a quick overview of SAD. Object oriented analysis and design (OOAD) is more recent methodology. Some key points about SAD is

- Developed in the late 1970s by DeMarco, Yourdon, and Constantine after the emergence of structured programming.

- In 1989, Yourdon published "Modern Structured Analysis".

- The availability of CASE tools in the 1990s enabled analysts to develop and modify the graphical SAD models.

The philosophy behind SAD approach is:

- Analysts attempt to divide large, complex problems into smaller, more easily handled ones. "Divide and Conquer"

- Top-Down approach

- Functional view of the problem.
- Analysts use graphics to illustrate their ideas whenever possible

SAD comprises of multiple models as listed below:

- Essential model
- Behavioral model
- Implementation model

Key features of an environmental model are:

- Defines the scope of the proposed system.
- Defines the boundary and interaction between the system and the outside world.
- Composed of: Statement of Purpose, Context Diagram, and Event List.

Key features of behavioral model are:

- Model of the internal behavior and data entities of the system.
- Models the functional requirements.
- Composed of Data Dictionary, Data Flow Diagram, Entity Relationship Diagram, Process Specification, and State Transition Diagram.

Key features of implementation model are:

- Maps the functional requirements to the hardware and software.

- Determines which functions should be manual and which should be automated.

- Defines the Human-Computer Interface.

- Defines non-functional requirements.

Just like OOAD, SAD also uses graphical notations and other elements to model a system. These elements are as follows:

- Data flow diagrams

  - show relationships between processes, data flows, data repositories and external infulences beyond the system boundary in a graphical and structured manner

- Process specifications

  - structured english, decision trees or tables: they document in a precise and consice fashion the elementary processing operations performed by each functional primitive in a set of dfds

- Data dictionary entries

  - describe the nature of data flows and hold the process specifications

- Entity Relationship Diagram

A data flow diagram (DFD) is used to indicate the flow of data and set of possible paths for data flow. It does not show the flow of control. The key features of DFD are as follows:

- A way to model a real world situation and specifically processes

- Their main purpose is to communicate with the user, the analyst's understanding of the scope of the required system

- DFDs are expanded or decomposed into levels. (Functional decomposition)

- Shows flow of data not flow of control

- Shows set of possible paths (not what causes a path to be taken)

Various elements of a data flow diagram are as follows:

	Process

→	Data Flow

	Data Store

	Source/Sink (External Entity)

Process: Process is referred to as work or actions performed on data (inside the system). The naming for a process should be verb phases. Every process receives input data and produces output.

Data Flow: Data flow is a path for data to move from one part of the DFD to another. The direction of the arrow indicates movement of data. It can also represent flow between process and data store by two separate arrows.

Data Store: Data store is used in a DFD to represent data that the system stores. Labels should be noun phrases.

Source/Sink: These are external entities which are origin or destination of data (outside the system). It is the singular form of a department, outside organization, or person etc. The labels should be noun phrases.

An example of a full-blown DFD is as follows:

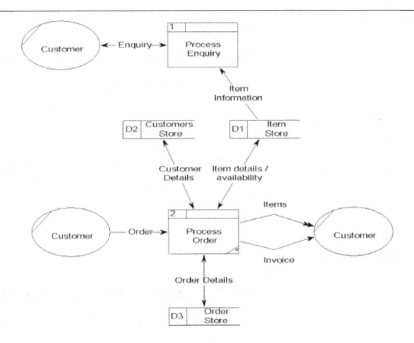

This image has been taken from https://commons.wikimedia.org/.

Data flow diagrams (DFD) levels

Business processes are too complex to be shown on a single DFD, so we use decomposition. Decomposition is the process of representing the system in a hierarchy of DFD diagrams. Child diagrams show a portion of the parent diagram in greater detail.

The basic level DFD diagram is also known as Context Diagram. There are other levels of the diagrams, each level of diagram shows more granular level of information as far as processes are concerned. So the context diagram shows the high level processes, whereas level 1 shows the process steps for each processes in context diagram.

Context Diagram

- Shows the system and the external entities with which it interacts

Top Level Diagram

- Shows the main processes in the system - a decomposition of the context diagram process

Lower Level Diagrams

- Decomposition of the processes in the top level - can be successively decomposed

Some key aspects of different levels of DFD are as follows:

- If a process p is expanded, the process at the next level are labelled as p.1, p.2 etc.

- All data flow entering or leaving p must also enter or leave it's expanded version

- Expanded DFD may have data stores

- No external entity can appear in expanded DFD

- Keep the number of processes at each level less than 7

Balancing involves insuring that information presented at one level of a DFD is accurately represented in the next level DFD.

Steps for creating DFDs

Context diagram

- Draw one process representing the entire system (process 0)

- Find all inputs and outputs that come from or go to external entities; draw as data flows.

- Draw in external entities as the source or destination of the data flows.

Level 0 diagram

- Combine the set of DFD fragments into one diagram.

- Generally move from top to bottom, left to right.

- Minimize crossed lines.

Level 1 diagram

- Each use case is turned into its own DFD.

- Take the steps listed on the use case and depict each as a process on the level 1 DFD.

- Inputs and outputs listed on use case become data flows on DFD.

- Include sources and destinations of data flows to processes and stores within the DFD.

- May also include external entities for clarity.

Ideally, a DFD has at least three levels. *When the system becomes primitive i.e. lowest level is reached and further decomposition is useless.*

Index

Notes

Notes

Made in the USA
Middletown, DE
16 February 2023